Container Gardening for Beginners

ESSENTIAL BEGINNER'S GUIDE TO ORGANIC GARDENING: GROWING VEGETABLES, FRUITS, HERBS, EDIBLE FLOWERS, AND ORNAMENTAL PLANTS IN POTS, TUBS AND OTHER CONTAINERS

JORDAN BRYCE

TABLE OF CONTENTS

CHAPTER - 13
HOW HYDROPONIC GARDENING WORKS

Introduction

Container gardening can be referred to as the growing of plants such as fruits, herbs, and vegetables in containers. It is an ideal practice for people living in high-rise apartments who do not have access to outside spaces. This system of gardening also works fine for people with a limited budget that can't afford to maintain a regular garden.

Container gardening can be used in creating a stylish simple garden space using high or low maintenance, depending on what works for you. It is ideal for people who find it difficult to bend down due to old age or any other health challenges. Setting large containers of 2 or 3 feet high, on the ground makes it easier for you to reach and makes the plants less prone to weeds, unlike conventional gardens. With this system of gardening, you can create an attractive planting design quickly, which will, in turn, become a center attraction.

When you read the word "container" you might think that you cannot possibly restrict your gardening dreams to some sort of large tub or to an array of various pots and vessels. However, you shouldn't take a limited view of container gardening at all. This is because containers can be almost anything.

Just consider that a gallery of images relating to modern container gardens might include:

- 5-gallon plastic buckets modified as self-watering vessels;

- Children's plastic swimming pools;

- Old parts of gutter;

- Traditional "half barrels" made of wood;

- Formally constructed patio planters in a range of shapes and sizes;

- Hanging baskets and formally made hanging planters (such as the upside-down tomato gardens that are all the rage);

- Any sort of "found" vessels that can contain soil, drainage materials, and provide good growing conditions - such as old wheelbarrows, old plastic barrels, etc. and

- The many types of "official" pots available.

In these vessels you can easily grow everything from the simplest array of herbs and greens to complex items like citrus trees, different types of fruits, and even some larger plants such as a single stalk of Brussels sprouts or an ongoing head of crisp celery.

Fundamentally you are only limited by a few factors. These are:

- Your imagination;

- The conditions you have available;

- The space you have available; and

- The money you can commit to purchasing seeds, plants, and materials.

Once you learn what a plant needs in order to grow and thrive in a container, it becomes easier and easier to spot containers good for your preferred plants, and to continue making plans for growing a diversity of food. Yes, there are limitations in container gardening, but there is also a great deal of opportunity.

As an example, container gardening can be a very orderly practice that is done on the rooftop of an apartment building using formally constructed wooden planters and clay pots.

However, a container garden can also be a total success for someone with a single, large and sunny window in their apartment's living area. The garden could be designed like a series of shelves across the window and contain a tremendous number of plants that produce food year-round!

So, as you begin to learn about the needs of container grown foods, be sure to keep in mind that there are very few other rules apart from a plant's need for sun, water, good soil and drainage, and pollination if it is a "fruiting" plant. Once you understand if these things are possible with your location and materials, you can begin making your own unique container garden.

Keep in mind that you can also use container gardening to grow your own flowers for the table, and you can even use "companion" planting to give all of the plants the kinds of ideal conditions that lead to extremely abundant harvests. You can also go entirely organic, use homemade compost to enhance the health of your plants, and even experiment with hydroponics if you are willing to invest in the supplies.

In-home and container gardening is one of the broadest ranges of gardening methods around. You have a lot more control when you use containers, and this means you can get almost guaranteed results - even without any sort of green thumb.

Chapter - 1
AN INTRODUCTION TO VEGETABLE GARDENING

Vegetable gardening includes choosing a site, planning the garden, preparing the soil, selecting the plants and seeds, planting a crop, and cultivating the plants until they are ready for harvest. The final result is new produce to consume, share, or market.

Anyone who's willing to spend some time daily or 2 to nurture the crops may grow a vegetable garden. It does not take a good deal of cash, time, or ability, though some of each will be useful. With practice and patience, your abilities will improve each year. Do not be discouraged if the first effort is not a massive success.

Growing veggies takes Some distance, but not always acres. A vegetable garden may be in the floor or within a planting bed, however it does not need to be. Many vegetables can be raised in containers. By way of instance, sufficient lettuce for a salad could be raised at a 12-inch kettle on the rear deck. Insert several radishes and carrots, also raised in 12-inch containers, like sweetness and spice, and you get a fantastic start on a yummy salad.

Vegetable gardening is one of our species' oldest jobs. Humans first started exploring and practicing agriculture around 9500 BCE, or more than 11,000 years ago. It was this discovery, that not only does the ground produce food, but we are also able to control that production, which allowed us to start forming villages, towns and eventually cities.

Agriculture brought many advances. Medicines could be grown; ancient Egyptians began to use plants like aloe Vera as medicines. Agriculture also paved the way for us to start producing textiles like cotton or hemp. But none of these discoveries hold a candle to vegetable gardening. Before the discovery of agriculture, it wasn't uncommon for tribes of humans to be starved throughout the winter; great swaths of the population were often wiped out due to lack of food. Being able to control the production of food allowed us to make enough food to store throughout the winter and avoid starvation. It absolutely changed the future of mankind; we went from being primitive animals to inventing the written word so that these practices could pass down from generation to generation.

The switch into agricultural practices created a new way of living. For centuries to come, being a farmer would be seen as a noble tradition. Often discriminated against due to the laws of the ruling class, these hardworking individuals kept the kingdoms and villages supplied with food. Despite all the hardships, vegetable farmers were a necessary part of the human equation.

It wasn't until the emergence of nowadays' modern man that vegetable gardening and farming started to get a bad rap. With all the new technologies that are invented every day and the fact that you can go to the grocery store and find any vegetable you want; the concept of vegetable gardener and farmer have begun to seem less appealing to the average person. Now, instead of learning how to garden, young adults are heading off for an education in law or business. Others would look towards fame and fortune, either succeeding or burning out along the way.

As the twentieth century came to an end, it seemed as if vegetable gardening as a career, hobby, or even an interest was fading away, just another feature of the distant past that no longer concerned mankind as it moved into the future. When you can order your food online and chemical treatments produce vegetables twice the size they were in the past, it seemed clear that getting your hands dirty in the soil was no longer needed.

But the twenty-first century has seen this reversed. As man has created more technology and automated more and more processes, there has been a fatigue that has cropped up. People have started to get tired of all of the chemicals being pumped into their food; they are no longer as appealing as they once were. There has been a movement towards embracing green or environmentally sound practices, as well as a push towards organic foods that are free of harmful chemicals.

The twenty-first century man has found that returning to the soil is a peaceful experience. There is a sense of pride in growing your own food, a feeling of doing something that matters and getting back to the roots of what it means to be a human, by taking part in and sharing an experience that has connected human beings together for more than four hundred generations.

Chapter - 2
PLANNING YOUR ORGANIC VEGETABLE GARDEN

Planning your vegetable garden might not sound like the most fun part of the process, and you'd be right to think so. At this stage you don't even get your hands dirty. There are considerations of space and logistics which need to be considered, and these can be pretty boring to figure out. But by planning your garden properly, you will be equipped with all the knowledge you need to have in order to understand exactly what conditions your plants are growing in. Just because it is boring, it doesn't mean it has to be hard.

The second part will be where the planning actually gets pretty fun. Once you understand the factors of the first half, it is time to start picking and choosing which vegetables you are going to grow. We'll highlight a handful of veggies during this part and cover some basic planning tips.

Deciding Where to Plant Your Garden

If we are going to be starting a vegetable garden, then the very first thing that we need to do is pick a location for our vegetable garden.

It's easy enough to look out your window at your backyard and say you've got it figured out, but it really isn't that simple. In your backyard, there are dozens of places in which you could plant your garden depending on how you space it or position it, and also the size of your backyard. Each possibility is technically in your backyard, but locations aren't all made the same. Some are better than others and some are downright unsuitable for gardening.

In this stage of your planning, you should take a moment to consider each of the following environmental attributes. Some of these you can tell just by looking at your yard, but others will require a little bit of data gathering. These steps are included where necessary. You can get by with growing in a location that is a little less than ideal for some of these attributes, but spots which fail on multiple fronts are best avoided.

Elevation: This one can usually be done through eyesight alone. Looking at the space you are thinking about planting your vegetables, is it elevated? Is it on an incline? Is it at the bottom of an incline? Is it rather flat? Depending on which of these questions is the most accurate, you are going to have a unique relationship to watering your plants. Generalized advice on watering your plants assumes that they are in a flat space. Plants that are on an incline will act flat. Plants on the bottom of an incline are going to need less water. Those planted on an elevated surface will require more water than normal.

Sunlight: Plants need a certain amount of sunlight a day. Some species prefer this light to be direct, others prefer it to be indirect, in the shade. Some want as much sun as possible, while others need relatively little direct sunlight. If you are going to be growing vegetables, then you are going to need to know two things. You are going to need to research the species of plant to see how much sunlight it needs, and you are going to need to know how much sun your chosen space gets. Keep an eye on the space throughout a day and see how much time it is in the sun and in the shade. Finding this out will let you know which vegetables will do best in this particular space. If you are looking to plant some veggies that want a lot of sun and some that don't want much, then remember that you don't need to grow everything in the same bed. It is better to grow multiple beds than try to force a plant out of its comfort zone.

Coverage: How much foliage or coverage from rain and wind does the space have? Are plants going to be safe from high winds where you plant them? Are they going to be able to get enough water when it rains or is the foliage going to misdirect it? Flipside, is the foliage going to help to prevent drier plants from drowning? Coverage isn't necessary when it comes to vegetable gardening, but many gardeners have no choice but to work with it because of having trees in their backyards or limited space.

Security: How safe are your vegetables? Vegetable farming doesn't tend to bring out thieves the same way that cannabis or fruit farming does. Well, at least not human thieves. Vegetable farming does bring out mice, rabbits, deer and other herbivores. While seeing a deer eating your vegetables is a good sign (after all, it means they must be pretty tasty), it also means that you now have a half-ruined crop. If there is easy access to your backyard or growing space, then you should consider how you can add some security to prevent unwanted visitors. This can be as easy as adding a knee level plastic fence around the garden but if you can offer security in one direction (such as when growing next to a house) then you can save money by using less fencing and limiting critters from approaching.

Ease of Access: This is the one factor that causes the most problems, but new gardeners don't realize it until it is too late. When you are first planning out your garden, it is easy to forget about the fact that you are going to need to be able to maneuver through it. Maintaining your crops requires you to water each plant and inspect it for signs of problems. If you plant your crops in such a way that you can't get easy access to some of them, then you are going to end up neglecting those plants and they will reflect this in their yield. Most gardeners get a pack of vegetable seeds and then plant them too close together. When the plant you are growing is so tiny to begin with, it is easy to forget what size they are going to be growing to. This is the reason that crops are most often planted in rows. Try to keep size in mind and ensure that there is enough space for you not only to get at every plant but to be able to get down and inspect each one.

Ground or Container: The majority of this book is written under the assumption that you are growing your plants in the ground itself. At this stage, it is important to note that, while there are some general differences between these two methods, there are also many similarities. Whether you are growing containers that are above ground or below ground, they tend to need to be watered more often than plants grown outside of a container. Beyond this main difference, they will still require as much sunlight, security and ease of access as any other garden bed you plant.

Putting It All Together: Once you have considered each of these attributes of the space, you can decide if it will be a good fit for your plants or not, as determined by their needs. Figuring out each of these attributes will take time and make it a longer wait before you are ready to plant your vegetables, but it can save you from some nasty surprises that could lead to weak veggies and poor yield. A spot that looks perfect at first glance might not get enough sunlight or shade for the plants you were looking to put there. Knowing this ahead of time allows you to match your garden to the local conditions so you can have the most productive vegetable garden possible.

Chapter - 3
HOW TO MEASURE YOUR GARDEN

The most important things you have to consider when choosing containers are your budget, what type of plants you want to grow and where you will grow them. If you are going to grow shallow root crops like onions, you will only need small containers that are about 6-10 inches in size. If you want to add succulent vegetables which need more root space, you will have to invest in 5-gallon containers. Plastic containers are the cheapest ones available. There are also containers made out of wood, but it is best to avoid them, as they might be treated with chemicals, which may eventually leak and get into your plants and eventually into your food. Ceramic containers are the best containers to use, although they are also the most expensive. Whatever material you choose, though, just make sure that they have suitable drainage.

For vegetable gardening, you don't need just a container. You need an appropriate one. You can't just randomly use any pot or container to grow any type of plant. Vegetables with petty roots can grow in shallow containers. But you should not use similar containers for deep rooted plants and root vegetables like beet, carrot and potatoes. In case of root vegetables, the thumb rule of selecting containers is selecting those which allow space to double the size of root vegetables. Since the size of potatoes generally ranges between 4 - 7cm, the apt container for the job would be of depth of at least 14 - 15cm. Container of this dimension can't be used to grow carrot. For that you need some 50cm deep container.

While medium rooted vegetables like herbs, tomatoes, salad greens, peas and beans need shallow space to grow well. Containers that can carry apt and minimum soil to make available required level of moisture and nutrients are best for the job.

The size and number of containers that you need will depend upon the amount of space that you have available for your container garden. The important thing is that the space should have access to at least 6 hours of direct sunlight everyday (or 4 hours, depending on which plants you choose to grow). Ideally, your garden should be at a vicinity which you pass by every day, so that you won't accidentally neglect your plants. A water source should also be close by.

If you can, find a 24-inch container which can serve as your all-around container garden. This size can fit a large vegetable plant such as a tomato, eggplant or pepper, as well as allow you to grow tall plants such as okra or fennel. The extra space around the edges can be used for planting smaller herbs or greens such as lettuce or spinach.

If you have the tiniest bit of space available, you might want to consider a themed garden, such as planting vegetables and herbs that you use to create specific types of dishes. For instance, you can create an Italian cuisine vegetable and herb garden.

For those of you whose available garden space gets only 4 hours of direct sunlight, your best option would be to grow a salad garden full of leafy vegetables such as a lettuce, Swiss chard, and spinach. Root crops such as carrots, beets and radishes, will also fare well in this set-up. Just keep in mind that this type of garden will require a lot of organic compost and, eventually, more constant watering.

Now that you have gathered your containers and assessed your garden space, you can now move forward to another fun part of the planning, and that is to choose the vegetables and herbs that you can grow.

Chapter - 4
HOW TO PREPARE THE SOIL

Although traditional gardening and container gardening may bear some similarities, understand that the soil for container gardening needs to be well aerated. It should have proper drainage and can retain the moisture that the plants need to survive.

No matter how good your garden soil is, it is recommended not to use it alone in a container garden. When used alone, both aeration and drainage are affected which results in poor plant growth or no growth at all.

Soils used for container gardening should be modified to meet the required aeration and drainage. Soils that gardeners commonly used for containers are often referred to as artificial media or soilless because they contain no dirt. They are usually composed of various materials such as vermiculite, peat moss, coir fiber, and bark.

You need to slightly moisten the soil before planting if you prefer to use artificial media. Fill your container with soil, pour enough water, and lightly fluff the soil to dampen it evenly.

You can use garden soil, but you need to modify it first. An ideal soil-based mix is one part each of garden soil, perlite, and peat moss.

Advantages and Disadvantages of Soilless and Modified Garden Soil

Modified garden soil is heavier than soilless media. It can provide the needed weight which allows the containers to keep upright during windy days especially if your garden is located outside your house. Soilless media may not be able to provide the needed weight to keep the pots in place.

Modified garden soil cannot guarantee that you will be able to get a disease-free soil for your garden. Your garden soil may contain weed seeds, harmful organisms, and pests that can harm your plants later on. Soilless media doesn't have such things and it is completely safe.

The garden soil is a lot cheaper than soilless media. A modified garden soil doesn't dry out fast and can hold the nutrients longer.

In terms of aeration, soilless media is the more suitable soil to use. You can also stretch it and fill more containers by adding and mixing some modified garden soil in it. But such practice may be risky because the garden soil could be infected with diseases. You can also reuse your soilless media year after year, provided that the plants that used the soil did not contaminate the soil with a disease. Using contaminated soil will only cause illness to your plants. Also, you may need to add fertilizer for added nutrients for your plants. It is also advisable to add compost.

Filling your Containers

When filling your containers with your chosen soil, avoid filling the container to the top. Allow a one-inch space between the rim of your container and the top of your soil. This will prevent the water from running over the edge.

Filling large containers is costly especially if you are using commercially prepared soil. To save some money, add some filler at the bottom of the container to take up the space. Just make sure that the roots of your plants will not lose the space they need while growing. In cases where the roots might touch the bottom of the container, it is wise to fill the whole container with soil. If you happen to have miscalculations and your plant outgrows the original container, then you should transfer it to a bigger one while you still can. You can also give it to someone who can provide the right area and enough room to grow.

Non-biodegradable items can be used as fillers such as small plastic jugs, crushed aluminum cans, and other packaging. Line a piece of landscape fabric above the filler and begin adding your soil. The fabric will keep the soil from invading the area of the filler while allowing the water to pass through without trouble.

Begin planting if there is already enough soil to hold the plant. Finish adding the soil until you achieve the required space between the soil and the rim of the pot. Use your garden tools when preparing your container garden to make things easier. Always keep your tools handy and in tip top shape. Don't strain your back and use your hand truck when transporting your filled containers.

Soil preparation can make or break your container garden. It is advisable to use the soilless media because it is safer and more suitable for your container garden.

Chapter - 5
BUILDING YOUR ORGANIC VEGETABLE GARDEN

How to Create a Container Garden

A container garden can be as simple or as complex as you wish. Once you learn how to choose your materials, what tools you need, and how to prepare your containers, you can get started.

Materials and Tools Needed

- Containers or pots
- Drill (if pot doesn't contain drainage holes)
- Potting soil
- Trowel

Containers come in all shapes, sizes, and materials. You can purchase containers, repurpose old gardening pots, use 5-gallon buckets, or invest in lightweight grow bags.

The size and depth of the container you use will depend on what plants you grow in them. Shallow-rooted plants (e.g., lettuce and greens) can grow in a space as little as 6 inches deep, but larger vegetables (e.g., tomatoes) require larger, deeper containers such as a 5- or 10-gallon pot.

Preparing and Modifying Containers

Getting your container ready for planting can mean simply selecting the pot and filling it with soil. However, there are other steps you should take to ensure you get the healthiest vegetables and have a positive experience.

1. Select your containers based on the vegetables you intend to plant. Take note of plant spacing and mature plant size to determine if multiple vegetables or herbs can grow in one pot.

2. If you're reusing gardening pots, wash them with a 10 percent bleach mixture to kill any pathogens remaining from a past crop.

3. Unless you're using grow bags, ensure the pot contains several drainage holes. If the pot doesn't have holes, drill several holes in the bottom. Beware of containers with self-contained drainage trays. During heavy rains, the water can fill the reservoir, and without the ability to drain, the saturated soil can kill your plants.

4. For containers deeper than 18 inches, you can place a smaller inverted pot in the bottom. This saves money (you use less soil) and reduces the weight.

Consider placing large containers on wheeled plant caddies, in case you ever need to change their location.

Filling Your Containers

For vegetables growing in containers, you need potting soil or potting mix. Garden soil (from your yard or in bags) should not be used because of its water-holding capacity and inability to drain well.

You can purchase bagged potting mix or mix your own (see here). If you choose a bagged mix, keep in mind that many nonorganic mixes contain synthetic fertilizer. If you choose an organic potting soil, you can add a granular, slow-release fertilizer, following the dosage instructions on the bag.

When you're ready to fill your container, leave only 1 to 2 inches of space at the top. The soil will compact, giving you more space for watering and mulch as the season progresses.

How to Build a Raised Bed Garden

You can find a myriad of options and plans for building a raised bed, but I'll share the most basic plan.

Preparing Your Site

The most important part of preparing your site is making sure it is level. Measure out the bed size and check its slope with a leveling tool. If there is any slope to the ground, you may need to scrape one side until the land is level on all sides.

If your ground contains pernicious weeds or grass, lay down an organic barrier, such as cardboard, to smother them. An alternative is to simply scrape the top layer of vegetation and turn it over; it will compost into the soil over time. If you think you may have rodents such as voles or moles, you will need a permanent barrier (hardware cloth, for example) because organic barriers will eventually break down into the soil.

Materials and Tools Needed

If you're willing to pay for convenience, purchasing raised bed kits is an option. But to save money and go the DIY route, you'll need these tools to construct a standard 4-by-8-foot, 10-inch-high raised bed:

- 3 (2-by-10-inch-by-8-foot) pieces of lumber (or 2 by 8 inches or 2 by 12 inches, depending on how tall you want your beds)

- Measuring tape

- Pencil

- Carpenter's square

- Circular saw or handsaw

- Drill or impact driver

- 12 (2½-inch) deck screws

- Roll of ¼-inch hardware cloth (optional)

- Staple gun (optional)

- Level

The most durable and budget-friendly wood is pressure-treated pine, widely available at home supply stores. However, there is a lack of research showing whether chemicals used in the treatment process leach into the soil and at what levels (if any) those chemicals are taken up by plants. You can check with your local home center or lumberyard to find out what rot-resistant natural wood options are available.

Building Your Raised Bed

Once you gather the materials, set aside a few hours to build your raised bed. Though it can be built by one person, an extra set of hands is always useful.

1. Take one 8-foot board and mark it with the pencil 4 feet from the end. Use a carpenter's square to draw a vertical line across the

board.

2. Cut the board at the vertical line with a saw.

3. Lay out the four pieces of board in the shape of a rectangle: the two 8-foot parts parallel to each other and the two 4-foot parts parallel to each other.

4. Situate one 8-foot board perpendicular to one 4-foot board, where their ends meet flush. Position the other corners of the raised bed the same way.

5. Using the drill, pre-drill the holes. Then, screw each of the four corners together where the boards meet, using three deck screws per corner.

6. If you're using hardware cloth to cover the bottom of the bed (this prevents ground-dwelling rodents from getting to your plants from underneath), spread the cloth over the bed, stapling it in place. If it doesn't cover the entire bed and you have to use two strips, make sure you have a 6-inch overlap between strips.

7. Carry the bed to its site and position it. Set the level on each of the four sides, ensuring the bed is level in all directions. If the bed isn't level, use a shovel to scrape down higher areas of dirt until the bed is level.

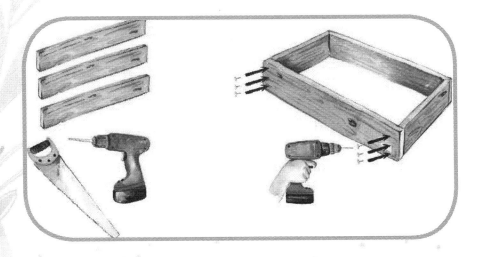

These plans can be modified for differing dimensions, but you should never exceed 4 feet in width. You want to be able to reach into the middle of the bed. If your bed will be next to a fence or other area, make it no wider than 3 feet. The length of the bed is up to you.

Many people prefer taller raised beds. For a bed taller than 12 inches, you will need more than one board for each side. In this case, each corner will need to be anchored by a 4-by-4-inch post, with each sideboard screwed into the post instead of into the perpendicular sideboard.

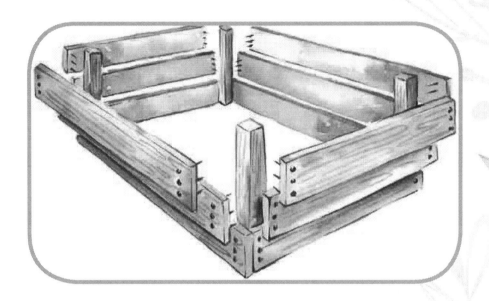

Filling Your Raised Bed

For a raised bed, you want a slightly "heavier" medium (soil mixture) than for a container garden. A higher proportion of topsoil and compost adds moisture retention and nutrients.

As you begin planting your vegetables, think about the orientation of your raised bed, especially in regard to larger and taller plants.

Plants that grow vertically or taller than others should be planted on the north, east, or northeast part of your raised bed. Lower-growing plants should go on the south, west, or southwest side. This way, tall crops, such as tomatoes or pole beans, do not shade shorter crops, such as peppers or sweet potatoes, from the much-needed southwesterly sun exposure. The exception is if you plan to grow cool-weather crops, such as greens, further into the summer. These crops benefit from afternoon shade and may grow longer before bolting if provided with shade. (For gardeners in the southern hemisphere, these cardinal directions will be opposite.)

How to Cover Your Garden

Most gardens will benefit from some type of covering to protect them from the elements during at least part of the year.

Floating row covers help gardeners begin their growing season earlier and extend it later. Air- and water-permeable covers made from lightweight polyester fabric protect crops from frost, allowing a few extra weeks of growing time on the bookends of the season. For in-ground gardens and raised beds, you can make arches with PVC pipe and lay the cover on top for a dome effect. Attach the cover to the PVC with clamps to ensure it doesn't blow off. For small plantings or for those in containers, placing upside-down plastic pots or cups on top of vulnerable plants works well. (Place a rock on top of the pot or cup to prevent it from blowing away.)

In some areas, wind damage is a major concern. Siting your garden on the south or southwest side of a structure or natural brush offers some protection. Well-anchored floating row covers can also protect lower-growing or young crops from wind.

Many gardeners find their biggest challenge isn't the cold or wind, but heat. Particularly in the southern United States, the recommended full-sun location might translate to stressed plants when temperatures rise to almost 100°F. In this case, afternoon shade can help sun-loving crops such as tomatoes and peppers. If you grow in containers, move them to a shady location in the heat of the day. If you grow in raised beds or an in-ground garden, use shade cloths in place of floating row covers (floating row covers trap heat; shade cloths allow air circulation).

For other conditions necessitating extra protection, always consider your plants' particular needs when deciding how to best cover your garden.

Chapter - 6
GROWING VEGETABLES FROM SEEDS OR PLANT

What to Sow

Before you can purchase your seeds, you need to decide what you can grow. This will depend on multiple factors, but the main ones being your local temperature zone as taught by the USDA and the season. For instance, if it is summer you can grow tomatoes but not asparagus. If you live somewhere with a short growing season, such as up north, you will also need to take this into account. In this case, you may have to start your seeds indoors prior to the beginning of the season and then transplanting them outdoors after the last frost. Although, not all crops can be started inside, as peas, beans, and root vegetables do not handle transplantation well.

Choosing Your Seeds

When purchasing seeds, you don't want to use anything lying around. Instead, choose to purchase from reputable suppliers. These companies should run germination tests, and some may even run a variety of trials to ensure the highest quality. This greatly affects seeds, as higher quality seeds are more likely to sprout, sprout more quickly and produce stronger seedlings which can hold up to transplantation and slight weather shifts.

While you can buy seeds online, another and often better option is to find seeds that you know are well-adapted to your local region. You can do this by going to local seed swaps where you may offer to buy seeds if you have none to trade or from regional suppliers.

When possible, it is best to purchase heirloom seeds rather than hybrids. These have many benefits, but many people choose them simply because their flavor is superior to that of hybrids, as while developing hybrid seeds manufacturers often sacrifice both nutrition and flavor. Another benefit of heirloom seed is that they are open-pollinated, which means that you can save seeds to plant for years down the road. This is a wonderful ability as if you plant a hybrid vegetable you are unable to remove the seeds from the harvest to use again in the future.

Timing

When beginners are starting their gardens, they don't want to wait. But this leads to many people who are starting their plants from seeds starting too early. While it is a good idea to start your seeds outdoors, if you do it too long before you are able to transplant the seedlings outdoors then they can become weak and root bound. This is a problem as the seedling will then have difficulties once outdoors. On the other hand, if you start your seeds too late then you will miss the best time of the season for growth. Therefore, follow the directions for your specific seed and temperature zone. There is no one rule for this, as it varies based on your location and plant type.

Soil

Just as the soil in your garden bed is important to be well-balanced, it is of equal importance to have proper soil to start your seeds in. You want soil that can drain well to prevent roots from rotting. Using a soil blend with peat or coconut fiber (coir). While peat is a more traditional option, it is being used less now as it has an extremely slow growth rate and is difficult to harvest. However, coconut fiber has the same texture as peat moss but stays hydrated better. Coconut fiber is also much easier to produce and harvest.

When planting your seeds, you can use a high-quality soil from the garden center, or you can make your own with one part each of high-quality soil, coconut fiber, and compost. When starting your seeds in these you can place the prepared soil mixture in either recycled egg cartons or plastic seed starters supplied at gardening and hardware stores.

Food and Water

Three to four hours before you begin planting your seeds pour the prepared soil mixture into a large bucket or bowl. Add just barely enough water to moisten the soil mixture and then stir it together until uniform. Add the moist soil to your seed starting containers. You don't want to water the seeds as soon as you plant them, as the water may dislodge them. By first watering the soil you can give the seeds a chance to take hold before risking watering them.

After the three to four hours have passed, add two to three seeds to each of the prepared seed containers. You will need to follow the directions for the individual seeds regarding the depth they must be planted at. As soon as the seeds are covered in the recommended amount of soil cover the containers with either a plastic dome or plastic wrap. This will allow the seeds to have enough moisture to germinate.

As soon as sprouts begin to emerge in the following days, remove the plastic from the top of the container. Whenever the soil in the containers is dry to the touch gently water with a mister or spray bottle. You will also want to use organic fertilizer such as fish emulsion once the first leaves appear on the seedlings.

Prevent Disease

If you give your seedlings too much humidity and moisture, they can develop a fungal disease, known as damping off. You can aid in preventing this condition by adding in a half-inch of light-colored sphagnum moss to the top of your prepared soil mixture. This moss can absorb up to twenty times its weight in water, acts as an aeration source for young seedlings, and contains beneficial bacteria that prevent fungus and disease. One study conducted at the University of California concluded that by using sphagnum moss in planting seeds you can prevent an average of eighty to ninety percent of damping off diseases.

Keeping Warm

For seeds to germinate and sprout, they need a temperature of between seventy- and ninety-degrees Fahrenheit. Yet, most homes are unable to provide this type of warm constantly throughout the winter. Therefore, if you are trying to start your seeds indoors before spring begins you may want to purchase an electric germination mat. These an average cost forty dollars USD and are placed beneath the container of soil and seeds to provide the ideal temperature.

Light Exposure

Just as plants outdoors need sun exposure, you need to ensure that your seedlings get plenty of light, as well. However, seedlings require lighter than most homes can provide during the late winter months. Thankfully, you don't have to go out and buy expensive grow lights, as regular fluorescent lights will do the right. Simply use lamps with fluorescent bulbs and suspend them no more than an inch above the seedlings. You will need to adjust the position of the light bulbs as the seeds grow so that it remains one inch away. The seedlings will require fourteen to eighteen hours of solid light daily, which you can easily provide by buying a simple timer for your electrical outlet.

Encourage Strong Growth

You don't want your seedlings to suffer from a lack of root space, water, or nutrients. Therefore, after the sprouts are established and growing well, you will want to pinch and pluck away the weakest of the seedlings in each container. As each small container has two to three seeds this means you will need to remove one to two sprouts in each container. By doing this, you are ensuring that the strongest of the seedlings can grow strong and flourish. As the seedlings grow lightly brush your hand over the tops daily. You want to do this gently as to not overly disturb the seedlings, but enough to lightly jostle the stems. This practice stimulates the effects that wind provides and promotes stems to grow sturdier and stronger. If your seedlings begin to outgrow their containers before you can transplant them outside, then immediately move them into larger containers.

Transplanting

Seedlings should be ready to be transplanted into your garden bed or outdoor container after four to six weeks. You can help the seedlings by making this transition as easy and painless as possible. In order to do this, you can keep the seedlings in a covered outdoor location (such as a porch or open garage) during the daytime before bringing them inside in the evening. After the first day begins slowly moving the seedlings to a more brightly lit area to prevent sunburn.

This process should take about a week. Once the seedlings are fully adjusted to being outdoors during the day, known as hardening off, then you can transplant them to your prepared soil.

In order to give your seedlings, the best chance of success, you will want to ideally transplant them on a moderately cool and overcast day. If it simply won't stay cool outside, perhaps you live in the south, then you will want to wait and transplant the seedlings in the evening after the heat of the day has passed.

Before you begin transplanting the seedlings, give them a light watering one to two hours before you get to work. Once you are ready to transplant your seedlings, you want to gently tap the flat bottom of the containers on the ground, this will help the soil loosen. Then, use a trowel and gently remove the seedling and a little of the soil surrounding it form the container and place it in a prepared hole in the garden. Pat some soil over any remaining holes, leaving the plant level with the ground.

Propagating Cuttings

While you will likely be purchasing partially grown plants or seeds, not all plants can be grown from seeds. There are many perennial plants which are best grown when propagated from cuttings. This is especially beneficial if you particularly like the mother plant, as the new plant grown from the cutting will be genetically identical. This means that it will share the same qualities, such as color.

The season in which you need to take cuttings, the area you need to cut, and the length of cutting all vary based off the type of plant you are using.

However, there are a few tips that may help you no matter the plant type. These include:

1. Use clean cutting shears.

2. Do not cut a portion of the plant that has flower buds or flowers, as the nutrients within the plant needs to go to the root.

3. When you take your cutting do so in the early morning while it is fully hydrated.

4. Keep cuttings in a cool and moist place until you plant them.

5. Use a rooting medium that provides good drainage and aeration with low fertility. You can combine your own with equal parts of coconut fiber (coir) and perlite.

6. After cutting, dip a piece of the plant into an organic rooting hormone, which will promote the growth of roots.

7. After you have dipped the cuttings in rooting hormone, place them one-third to one-half of an inch into the prepared rooting medium with the tips point upward into the air.

8. Water the cuttings and then place the container in indirect sunlight. You want to avoid full sunlight.

9. Keep the cuttings in humid conditions with a clear plastic dome or a plastic bag placed over the container.

While there are different cutting recommendations based on the source plant, one of the most common types of cuttings you can take are stem cuttings.

When taking a stem cutting you want to find a plant free of disease and insects, plus the stem you cut from needs to be free of flowers and buds. Using a sanitized pair of gardening shears cut a three to a six-inch portion at a forty-five-degree angle. Cutting at this angle increases the rooting area. You want your cutting to include at least two or three leaves and the tip of the stem.

Chapter - 7
PROPERLY PLANTING YOUR ORGANIC VEGETABLE GARDEN

Start with the containers

Make a final check to ensure that the insides of each container are clean and free of debris. Also, closely inspect them for cracks. You want to find them now before you put them into use. Once you place your soil and plant in them, the increased weight and pressure will find these discrepancies for you.

Next, check your soil

This might sound simple, but make sure that you have more than enough for your containers. Leaving plants lying around, even in the shade, while you make a last-minute trip to the store puts them under stress.

Check for moisture

Soil needs to have the right consistency of moisture before you use it. While it does not require you to saturate it with water, it does mean is that it needs to contain more moisture than the bone-dry consistency that it presents when it is brought home in the bag. Using soil that is too dry when you plant will be hard to balance after planting. The roots will be feverishly searching the soil for any signs of moisture. Waiting until after it is planted to water it will stress the plant. It will also be much more difficult to balance the moisture level throughout the soil after planting has occurred.

The best approach to moisturizing soil is to place the amount of soil that you need in a bucket. Add a small amount of water to the soil and mix it until it is sufficiently damp. This means that it contains enough moisture that it is wet, but there should not be any patches where the soil is densely packed together because of a high concentration of water. Continue adding a small amount of water to the container until all of the soil is saturated.

Prep the plant

If you went with a seedling, your plant will already have a formed ball of soil packed around its root system. It is imperative that you do not try to pull this off. Attempting to do so could easily damage the roots and jeopardize the health of the plant.

Your plant's root ball will also probably contain small round pellets. These pellets are fertilizer the grower has used and are not a reason for concern.

In order to transplant the seedling, you first need to inspect it. Take a good look at the soil surrounding the root ball. If it is rather dry, you will want to add some moisture to it before planting- even if you have moistened your soil in the container.

Place the seedling in a small container of water and allow it to absorb some of the water into the root ball. It doesn't need to float in water or the soil surrounding the root ball will begin to loosen and break apart.

Move the plant

Once the seedling's root ball has received a sufficient amount of water, it can be transplanted into the new container. If the seedling's soil was sufficiently wet, then all that is necessary now is to transplant it from its original container to the new one. Since these seedlings are very delicate, it is important that you take your time when removing them from their old container.

Even though most seedlings will be small, it is common for some people to simply pull them out of their old container. This is the wrong thing to do. Pulling on the trunk of the seedling will cause it to snap in two or, at the very least, crack the trunk of the plant, which could eventually kill it.

The preferred method of removal is to place the seedling's trunk between the second and third fingers of one hand and turn the container upside down. Grasp the bottom of the container with your free hand and gently shake it to loosen the seedling from its container. In some instances, the plant may be lodged in tightly, so it might become necessary to tap the bottom in order to move it.

It is possible the plant will still resist moving from the old container. If this occurs, take a butter knife and slide it around the inside of the container on all sides between it and the plant. This should free the seedling.

Inspect the root ball

Depending on how long the plant has been allowed to grow in its old container, it is possible that it has established quite an elaborate root system. In fact, there are times when you remove a plant and all you will see is a twisted heap of roots with no visible soil. This means that the plant was allowed to remain in its container for far too long. While the plant can still be used, it will need some additional help in order to get started.

When roots are densely packed together, you will need to separate and loosen them somewhat in order to allow them to get a head-start once they are placed in the new container.

If you leave them in a mangled mess, the plant will probably still grow, but it will take longer for the roots to realize that they are no longer constricted in a small place. Helping them out speeds up the process.

You will want to gently loosen the roots of the seedling by pulling them apart. Stay away from the base of the plant as you can easily pull roots off the plant base, injuring the plant. Pry the roots apart as much as you can and then plant.

If you see that the root ball is densely packed with soil, you can also help this situation by taking your butter knife and making some small incisions in different places in the soil to loosen it up. The marks do not have to be deep and several small ones are much better for the plant than one or two large ones. Digging into the root ball too deep with a knife can damage roots deep down that you will not be able to see.

Plant your plants

Your new container should be filled with soil up to approximately one to one-and-half inches from the outer rim. Take your trowel or even your hand and remove a small amount of soil form the middle. Now, place the plant in the hole and pack the soil back around the plant while holding it upright.

You have to be very careful when packing soil around the plant as several things can happen. First, you may have a tendency to push too hard around the plant in an attempt to firmly seat it in the dirt. In doing so, you can very snap off the plant at the ground or just below it. If you find that the plant isn't firm in the soil, gently remove the soil and the plant and dig a slightly larger hole and try again.

Never try to force the plant into the ground.

Second, is that you can end up with a plant that is buried too deep. You want the root system to be submerged, but not part of the trunk of the plant. Judge how high the soil needs to cover the plant.

Make sure that the plant is sitting straight so that there is less likely of a chance that it will tip over or grow at an angle. As it begins to produce vegetables, the added weight on one side could jeopardize the stability of the entire plant.

Watering

Surprisingly enough, this involves more than just dumping water on the plant. If water isn't distributed evenly, you take the chance that the plant will not receive valuable water in some parts of the soil. Since the plant has already been put under some stress through transplanting, it does not need the added stress of having to search for water, too.

When you water a new plant for the first time, the water is likely to drain through the soil very quickly since it has just been recently moved into the new container and hasn't had sufficient time to become packed. Even if the soil was moistened before the plant was planted, the soil still needs even more water in order to give the plant the best chance for survival.

If you dump water on the loose soil in the container, chances are very good that the soil will become saturated and the root ball will receive very little of the water. Why would this happen? Because the root ball is denser, and the water will be diverted to flow through the easy, loose soil instead.

Instead of flooding the plant with a large volume of water all at once, a better approach is to give the plant a slow, steady drink so that it will allow it enough time to seep into every area—including the roots.

To complete your planting, you will probably have to add a little more soil to the container. When water is applied to the plant, it will automatically compact some of the soil on the surface creating an indentation that needs to be filled. Some people also like to top off the surface surrounding the plant with mulch, sawdust, tree bark particles, landscape fabric or any assortment of other materials. This not only helps to keep precious water from evaporating, but it also serves as a barrier to help discourage the growth of weeds.

It is a good idea to label your plants with tags, so you know what varieties of each plant you are growing.

Chapter - 8
HOW TO CARE FOR GROWING PLANTS

Taking care of your container garden is pretty much the same as with taking care of plants planted in the ground. The only difference is plants grown in containers require more monitoring, especially when it comes to watering. Here are some more of the tips that you can follow to make sure that your container garden is always in perfect shape.

After planting your preferred fruits, vegetables, and herbs, you need to observe proper maintenance and care next. Taking care of your container garden is not difficult, but compared to a traditional garden, a container garden needs extra watering and feeding.

Watering

Most plants need frequent watering, unless otherwise stated like in the case of Mediterranean herbs. Potting soil quickly dries out especially during windy or hot weather. You may need to water your plants more than once a day if the weather becomes unbelievably hot. In some cases, you may need to add liquid fertilizers and you can use your watering can for that.

To check if your plant needs more water, insert your finger into the soil. If you feel that the soil within the first few inches from the top is bone dry, then you need to water your plant. Make sure that your water penetrates the roots of your plant.

Applying Fertilizer

There is a need to fertilize your plants every two weeks to make sure that they get the right amount of nutrients. Liquid fertilizer is the easiest to use because you only need to mix the fertilizer with water and pour it onto the soil down to the roots. An organic fertilizer is a wise choice.

Beware of Pests

Although a container garden is less prone to pests than a traditional garden, there is still a chance that an infestation might happen. If you notice the presence of pests, act immediately and remove possible sources of the pests. You can also apply neem oil on the leaves and stems of your plants to prevent the pests from invading your garden. The oil acts as a natural fungicide and pesticide. It also discourages the feeding of the pests.

Ample Sun Exposure

Plants need sunlight to thrive and grow, so make sure that your plants are getting the needed amount of light. In the absence of the natural light, you can use your artificial lighting that still makes photosynthesis possible.

Regular Pruning

Make your plants look fresh and lively all the time by pruning them.

Dead leaves can make your plant look dull and unappealing, so you need to remove the dead leaves right away. Spray the leaves with water to remove the dust.

Plants with Disease

If you suspect that a certain plant in your garden has a disease, it is best to isolate the said plant and try to cure it. If the condition becomes worse, then it is best to discard the plant as well as its soil. Using the contaminated soil of the dead plant will only cause problems later on

Chapter – 9
MAINTAINING AND HARVESTING YOUR ORGANIC VEGETABLE GARDEN

Maintenance

You will need to maintain your container garden the same way you would do so for an in-the-ground garden. You just must do so on a smaller scale. The drawback of planting in pots is that they will have lesser amounts of nutrients in the soil. They will also hold less water compared to garden beds. Because of this, you must make sure you maintain the water and nutrient levels in the soil. You will need to this on a regular basis. This will help the plants survive and grow healthy flowers and leaves. It will also make sure the plants produce edible vegetables. You should be aware of a few things you need to do to maintain your garden. This includes feeding the soil, avoiding soil compaction, and pruning or caging.

Feeding the Soil

Earlier we talked about how to prepare the soil with organic fertilizers such as compost and manure. Sometimes, though, this is not enough to keep the soil healthy. If this is the case, you will need to feed the soil. As with anything else, your plants will tell you if they are getting enough nutrients. If they appear weak or stunted, or if they are not yielding as many veggies as you expected, the soil might be losing nutrients.

If this is the case, you should feed the soil. I recommend using organic methods, just as when you prepared the soil. To do this, you will need manure or compost and a small garden fork. When the soil in the pot is moist, break up the upper layer (four to six inches) with the garden fork. Then, till (or mix) the compost or manure into this layer, again with the garden fork. When you are done, spread more on top of the soil. Then water the plant well.

You can also use store-bought plant feed. Garden centers have organic plant food for sale. You should try to use these if you can. Most of these kinds of feed should be mixed with water before you apply them. Then, when you water your plants, you are also feeding them.

Soil Compaction

Just like in a garden bed, it is important to prevent the soil in your pots from being compacted. One way this happens is by leaning your weight on the soil when you are gardening. This is more common in garden beds. Gardeners will kneel or walk on their beds, which crushes the soil underfoot. But it can happen in large planters as well. Be careful not to compact the soil in this way.

A more common way soil is compacted in pots is by watering. If you do not use a watering can that has a rose to break up the water, or if you do not use a nozzle on your hose that makes a fine mist, you risk pounding the soil into a hard crust. Of course, the best way to prevent this is by using the proper tools. But if you do not have these kinds of tools, there is another solution. You can place a broken pot or plate in the soil. Then, let the water flow onto the hard surface. This will lessen the force of the water before it touches the soil.

Before you water your plants, you should also break up the soil. You can do this with a fork or a trowel. Doing this will allow water and air to pass more easily to the roots.

Pruning and Caging

Many of your plants should not be left to grow however they want. You will have to control their growth with stakes, cages, or pruning.

Big, bushy plants like tomatoes, peppers, and squash need stakes and cages. This is true even if you are growing patio varieties. The cage or stake will support the plants. This will be especially important when they begin to produce their heavy fruit. Without a support structure, the fruit will drag the plant's branches to the ground. Place cages around tomatoes and peppers early. You will need to guide the plants up into the cage as they grow. This will be much easier than trying to force a cage over a plant that has already grown and is too bushy.

Pruning makes sure plants do not grow out of control. It also promotes the kind of growth you want. For example, you should prune tomato plants. You will want to pinch the stems that grow at 45-degree angles from the main stem. Leave the stems that grow at right angles to the main stem. The 45-degree stems take nutrients away from any tomatoes growing on that stem. Leaving them on will result in many tomatoes not becoming ripe. Talk to a master gardener about what kinds of pruning the other veggies in your garden need.

Harvesting

Harvesting time varies with each crop. For you to understand the ideal time to harvest and the best means of picking to avoid damaging. The followings are a few things you need to know:

- Check the seed packs to understand the harvest time better.

- Check the number of days to maturity.

- If you are a new gardener, keep a record in a journal to help you make notes on your observations.

- Record what you have planted and the date to know the time they would be ready for harvesting. It will help a lot pending when you familiarized yourself with each variety.

As a gardener, you will learn gradually to be patient and not harvest before crops are ready. For example, pumpkins might look big enough to pick and eat, but they are not good to reap until the stem dries off, turned hard and vines die out. If you pick them earlier, the seeds might not be adequately matured to keep. The taste as well would not be at its best. Cut the stalks at about 5cm from the fruit to increase storage time. Let the pumpkins dry-off in the sun for one or two days to make their skin tough. They have a long storage life if they are well stored.

Another example is beans. They can be picked while they are young or give them more days to be matured before harvesting so that you can get the best nutritional value out of them

The maturity times of beans varied with the variety you grow. Variety like runner beans is as short as six weeks and could keep producing for about four months. Variety like bush beans and climbing start producing at about nine weeks provide you with abundant harvest for about three months. Zucchinis are ideally harvested young (approximately 10cm long if they are to be pickled) since they grow faster in hot weather and could suddenly turn into a marrow.

Plants use a vast amount of their energy in fruiting and flowering. Thus, it is significant to ensure they acquire enough soil nutrients to assist them to produce plenty of crops, and also to build their immune system, making them more resistance to diseases and pests.

Bear in mind when harvesting crops like leafy greens, the best time to harvest them are late afternoon or early evening instead of morning to prevent eating avoidable nitrates in your food. The sunlight must have converted the nitrates in the daytime. Plants will discharge or share about thirty percent of the energy produced using photosynthesis in the day with the root area. This assists in feeding beneficial microbes that helpful to plant directly. While the microorganisms in turn discharge nutrients to the plants to keep growing.

Chapter - 10
STORING AND PRESERVING VEGETABLES AND FRUITS

S toring your harvest is the best means of dealing with the surpluses of your crops against season when little is growing. The different ways to store your vegetables include freezing, drying and preserving. Some vegetables and fruits store well for months if you keep them in the appropriate conditions. What is most important is selecting unblemished variety and inspect them frequently, taking out any contaminated items. For instance, one spoiled pear can damage the entire bunch. Storing the harvests in a dehydrated, well-ventilated environment would prevent them from decaying. You can use a shallow cardboard box or wooden crate as well as storage boxes. Whichever you are using, ensure it gives room for proper ventilation.

Pears and apples are suitable for storing. Cover each fruit in paper and put in separately in the base of your container. Root vegetables like beets, potatoes, and carrots also suitable for storing. Remove the leafy edge of the carrots and beets put them in the box separately without covering. They both have the advantage of being covered by a layer of sand, making them tough. Potatoes could be stored in paper sack or hessian. Harvest them on a dry day and allow drying in sun. Take away any mire from the potatoes to stop from forming mold. Store them in a dark area to prevent from forming poisonous green patches on the outer layer. Leave parsnips in the ground over the winter and harvest when you need them.

Shallots, Garlic, and onions are to be dried thoroughly and plaited before storing in a dry environment. The tops could also be removed and hang the bulbs in an old pair of netting or tights. Squash related plants like pumpkins can stay for about three months. It all depends on the type. Do not keep marrows and pumpkins after mid-winter. However, other squash like spaghetti and butternut can be kept till early spring. Make sure they are in perfect state and store them in a dry, cool area like in the cabinet. A crop like zucchini doesn't stay long but can be refrigerated for about three weeks.

Leafy plants like spinach and lettuce don't store well, and they are ideal to be eaten in a few days of harvest. Plant more often in the early fall for you to have something to harvest in the cold periods. Legumes like beans and peas could be blanched and frozen or dried for use in a stew.

Freezing Your Harvest

Freezing is an easy and quick means to preserve your harvest. Freeze in usable sizes so the frozen crops can quickly defrost when using. Select only ripe vegetables and fruits and freeze them immediately after harvesting. Put them in a plastic container or a sealed freezer bag to guarantee they are well kept and do not undergo freezer burn. Some vegetables and fruits will require blanching before freezing to prevent water in them rupturing and crystallizing their cell walls, leading to a soft consistency and boggy when defrosted. Just plunge the vegetable into a big bowl of boiling water at least $\frac{1}{3}$ of the normal cooking time, and move to chilled water, before patting dry and freezing.

The following freeze perfectly well:

- Gooseberries

- Rhubarb

- Cranberries

- Peas

- Blanched beans (these include French and runner)

- Blanched apples

- Blueberries

- Raspberries

Drying, Pickling and Bottling your harvest

Crops that dry better are apples, peppers, and tomatoes. Drying could considerably change the texture and taste of your products and could make appealing additions to meals. Just clean and thinly cut your vegetables and fruits and place the pieces in a single layer on a baking tray. You usually leave it outside or sun to dry it out. You can use your oven to dry it, put your oven to its minimum temperature set and place the tray inside for some hours until pieces have dried up. Following that, store the bits in a sterile airtight container and eat within one or two weeks.

Shallots and beets are tasty after pickled and can be kept for some months. Clean and prepare beets (do not take out the tops closer to the root, as it could lead to leaching out of color). Put in boiling water for about thirty minutes or until the heads and skins can be easily rubbed off. Cut them and put in a sterile jar and wrap in pickling vinegar. For shallots, peel and trim the bottom and tops. Put them inside a shallow plate and cover with salt to draw out surplus moisture. Leave them all night and clean carefully and put in a sterile jar then wrap with pickling vinegar.

Chapter - 11
VEGETABLES AND HERBS TO GROW ALL-YEAR ROUND

Cool Season Vegetables

Depending on the particular type of garden, a gardener may be interested in cultivating food sources during the colder season. Not all types of vegetable are cultivated during the summer and spring season because there as certain types of vegetables that can thrive very well in colder weather such as the following:

- Cauliflower

- Onions

- Mustard

- Leek

- Carrots

- Broccoli

- Spinach

- Kohlrabi

- Turnip
- Swiss Chard
- Leek

Cultivate these vegetables during both winter and fall and watch them grow. Because colder months yield lower temperatures, it will be unlikely for a gardener to apply any natural pesticides to their vegetables which even makes them organic and tastier.

Plant these winter vegetables close to a south-facing wall or other windbreak so that you can take advantage of the higher temperature as well as the protection to extend the growing season by a few weeks.

Warm Season Vegetables

Tomatoes

Tomatoes can be grown in tubs and pots, which give you easy access to one of the most common edibles in our different home recipes. They usually demand lots of nutrients supply for proper growth and frequent watering with much exposure to sunlight in order to get them well ripened. When growing your tomatoes, remember to choose a location with minimum sunlight exposure of 6 hours, although about 8 – 10 hours of sun is best for them. All varieties of tomatoes are suitable for container, but the determinate types (compact plants, bush plants or patio plants) are usually the best plants to grow in containers. They are very reliable and predictable because they set their flowers and fruits all at once, and they typically grow to a predetermined size (about 3 – 4 ft in height). The stockier bush and smaller tumbling varieties will not require pruning as they grow. You can plant a few marigolds alongside your tomatoes, as this will add color as well as produce a scent that helps to repel aphids. The variety of tomatoes planted should be relative to the size of the container used as they are very productive. You should also make use of a potting mix made up of some loam to help retain moisture for a longer time.

Beans

Beans are great and very productive when grown in containers. They are quite easy to grow, but also require enough sun and deep pots. The depth of the container usually depends on the plant variety. Bush beans require about 6 – 7 inches container depth while pole beans need about 8 – 9 inches of container depth. You are advised to use unglazed containers with good drainage to allow evaporation of excess water. Once your beans seeds germinate, which usually takes about 5 or 7 days, remember to conserve soil moisture by spreading mulch lightly over the surface of the soil. Beans require a well-drained soil mix with high organic content for healthy growth. You may have to grow pole beans close to a wall or provide them with long support like trellis, as they are climbers. It is advisable that if you're growing beans in a very large container, combine summer savory, kale, or celery with them. Inspect them regularly for insects, and don't wait too long before you harvest your beans else, they will become tough.

Squashes

These plants are best for rooftop or balcony. They are straightforward to grow and very productive in containers. They require large pots (at least 12 inches in height and diameter) but ensure they have one or more drainage holes to release excess water through. Make use of soil mix with good quality, tons of organic matter and good aeration. If you are planting seeds, fill the container with soil within 1 – 2 inches of the top while if you are growing from young plants, fill the container ¾ full. Sow 5 – 6 seeds in each container if you are growing from seed but cut back the plants to two after the seeds sprout. It is generally best to grow one squash plant in each container, and if you are staking your squash, do it before planting, right after filling the pot with soil. Squashes require 8 hours of sun exposure every day and should be protected from of frost and wind.

Find a perfect location in your garden where this requirement can be meant and remember to frequently water the soil to stay moist but not marshy.

Sweet Corn or Maize

Corn was at first the common name for oat crops like wheat, grain, oats, and rye. The excellent yellow grain we by and by considering as corn was familiar with Europe by Columbus and individual explorers. The corn plant conveys a tall stalk that yields a couple of ears each. Since corn requires a lot of nitrogen to thrive, it is commonly scattered 12 inches isolated. Regardless, if the corn is given good nitrogen, possible in an aquaponics system, corn can be planted as eagerly as every 6 inches, or four plants for each square foot.

Nearby Americans would plant corn, beans, and squash together and suggested these plants as the Three Sisters. The seeds would pump nitrogen into the soil. The corn would give a tall stalk to the bean plant to climb, and the squash leaves would shield the ground like mulch, with the prickly hairs on the vines ruining bugs. After the plants created, dishes combining beans and corn gave all-out proficient, diminishing the need to raise family unit animals for sustenance.

Chapter - 12
ALLIUMS AND HERBS

Basil

You'll want to grow this as similar to an annual or as a short-lived perennial in your container garden. Be sure to use a deep pot for this plant because it will require space for the roots. You also want a well-draining soil and don't water the pot unless it's dry.

Bay

Bay is something that will grow slowly at first, but it will eventually form a small tree or a bush that you can easily train into any shape you want. You should plant bay in a large pot with soil that drains well.

Chervil

This is also known as French parsley and is an annual that is very similar in appearance and taste, with some undertones of anise. In order to harvest this plant, snip the outer leaves and the stems. Be sure that this is in a soil that drains well and also water it regularly.

Chives

These plants look a lot like grass and are a perennial that has a slight onion flavor. They're a prolific producer in container gardens and have a mild taste. Cut off small bunches back to the soil level and allow the rest to

grow. Chives like soil that is slightly damp but be sure there is still adequate drainage. They're an excellent choice of plant for beginners.

Cilantro

Cilantro is also known as Chinese parsley and is a short-lived annual that has a citrusy, parsley flavor. It is better when you start it from the seed as it grows out quickly, but when it's harvested, it doesn't grow back.

Extend the harvest by growing a few pots in different stages. Cilantro also likes soil that drains well and well-aerated.

Dill

It's better when you grow dill indoors for the leaves because it will be hard to get it to seed and get a nice harvest. Sow a few pots at different intervals for a nice supply. Fernleaf is an excellent, compact variety that enjoys being grown in a container.

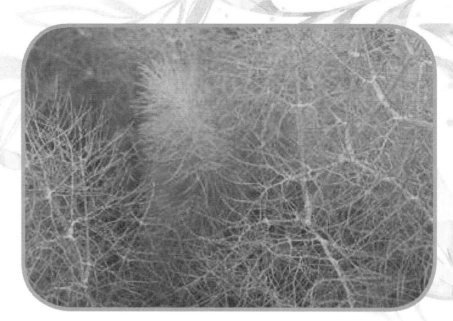

Marjoram

Marjoram comes from the Mediterranean area and is actually in the oregano family, but the flavor is a lot sweeter and more delicate. It's often grown in containers indoors.

Mints

Spearmint and Peppermint are great choices for container gardens when they are the only plant in the pot. They can easily take over the entire pot and should be planted alone. Be sure to keep the soil on the drier side.

Oregano

Oregano can easily grow to about a foot high in pots and has a spicy flavor. When you harvest the leaves, you encourage the plant to grow even more, and the plant will remain productive for up to two years. When the plant becomes woody, it should be replaced.

Parsley

Curly leaf and flat leaf parsley are excellent choices for growing inside containers both indoors and outdoors. The Italian variety is biennial and has a very robust flavor. When you harvest from the plant, cut the outer leaves. This encourages new growth at the center and keeps the parsley alive and productive.

Rosemary

Rosemary comes in two different forms, trailing and upright. The blue boy variety is compact and has a robust flavor, as well as the Salem or Taylor's blue. Even though this herb likes dry conditions, you shouldn't let the soil dry out completely since it will die.

Sage

You'll want to grow the twelve-inch dwarf sage for container gardening or a nonflowering variety like berggarten. Dwarf sage has the same flavor as garden sage but only gets ten to twelve inches high. Keep sage in a well-draining potting mix and fertilize it when needed.

Thyme

There are many different varieties of thyme, but the best ones for container gardening are the French thyme and the Lemon thyme. You can also try the oregano thyme, which is a trailing variety.

Ornamental

Most herbs can also be used ornamentally if you'd like, but there are some that have very beautiful flowers, an enticing aroma, and a deep green or unique foliage that adds a bit of flare to a container herb garden. Take a look at some of these ornamental herbs you could use to spice things up!

Silver Thyme

Silver thyme will get about twelve inches tall and has a lavender to pink blossom in the summer months. It's an evergreen that will need a twelve-inch-wide by twelve-inch deep pot in order to flourish. The fragrant, silver

leaves makes a bushy texture in the garden. It loves sunny locations and prefers a sandier soil. It's also an excellent addition to tea and sauces if you feel inclined to harvest it.

Oregano Blooms

Origanum leavigatum has a purple to pink blossom that blooms for a long time. It grows to about two feet tall and has dark green leaves with a purple tint. Unfortunately, these herbs are not very good for cooking, but they do have a beautiful scent and a nice appearance. Herrenhausen has masses of pink flowers that have maroon bracts on the purple stems while Hopleys is a taller plant with long-blooming, deep pink stems.

Roman Chamomile

Chamaemelum nobile is a one-foot tall plant with white blossoms that bloom all summer long. It's extremely aromatic with an apple to pineapple scent. The threadlike leaves can also be used in teas; the young leaves are the one you want to use for your tea. In the summer, the blossoms are white with an almost daisy-like appearance. This herb loves moist, rich soil and will grow to a foot tall in a proper pot.

Berggarten Sage

Also known as Salvia, this two-foot-tall plant blooms in the early summer and has violet to blue flowers. The foliage is compact, shapely leaves that are dark green in color. At two feet tall, it's perfect as a backdrop for shorter container plants in the front. The dusty green leaves are a beautiful background for almost any container garden. You can also use the leaves medicinally as a tea in order to treat throat and lung problems. This sage can also be used to flavor meats and potatoes.

Catmint

Nepeta X Faassenii is a herb that cats adore and is also known as catnip in many regions of the globe. It's an eighteen-inch tall, bushy plant when it's in the right conditions, and has lavender blossoms that will bloom all through the summer. It also attracts many beneficial insects to the garden with its blooms, so while it's not normally edible for people, it can be used in container gardens to attract bees and other small insects to pollinate vegetables.

Catmint light green foliage and should be cut back throughout the season to encourage it to bush out and blossom more.

Salem Rosemary

R o m a r i n u s officinalis 'Salem' makes a beautiful, two-foot long backdrop for many other plants that bloom. The blossoms on this herb are a nice blue color and it's an early bloomer in the spring, so it provides color where many herbs are not yet able to bloom. It's an evergreen that has green, shiny needle leaves that weave through the container like thread. You can prune it down to the level you'd like throughout the growing season and use the pieces you harvest in soups and stews after you've dried them.

This plant likes fertile soil, a lot of drainage, and plenty of sunlight.

Cardoon

Cardoon has a purple blossom that makes itself known in the mid-summer and grows to around five feet tall. Therefore, it's best planted on its own in a large pot to keep it happy. It has gray-green leaves that arch and frame in order to showcase the purple thistle-like flowers. This herb is also edible. The stalks and leaves can be blanched and consumed, as well as the unopened flower heads.

This plant prefers a sunny, well-drained area.

Sweet Cicely

Myrrhis odorata is a late spring bloomer with white flowers that grows around two to four feet tall. This is a shade tolerant herb that has a fernlike appearance that grows in a mound with bright-green leaves. In the late spring, it's topped with a white

star-shaped flower that has a shiny brown seed when it's finished. It does the best in partial to full shade in moist, rich soil.

The seeds and leaves have a sweet anise flavor that goes well with desserts, especially those made with fruits.

Anise Hyssop

This plant has a bright red bloom that appears in the late summer. The plant grows to about two to six feet tall, depending on the container it's placed in and has gray-green leaves. This plant prefers a well-drained, sunny area.

The flowers have an appealing taste, like a sweet anise, and it's delicious in salads. This is also another plant that's excellent for attracting bees and other beneficial insects to the garden.

Garlic Chives

Allium tuberosum have a white bloom that appears in the late summer. The plant grows to eighteen inches tall and prefers a sunny location with sandy, fertile soil. It also blends in well with its neighbors, like a flowering tobacco plant or some coneflowers. It has starry white flowers that catch the eye easily. After the flowers bloom, it's best to cut any of the seeds heads off and use them for decorative purposes because the seeds are vigorous growers. The flat, garlic-flavored leaves can be picked throughout the growing season in order to add to sauces, soups, and dips.

Now that you know the best herbs for different purposes in your container garden, let's look at the easiest ones to grow!

Chapter - 13
HOW HYDROPONIC GARDENING WORKS

How Plants Grow

Each plant is a natural workshop in the form of roots, stems, leaves, fruits, and seeds that create organic matter. A plant can take up any organic material; it absorbs inorganic mineral salts instead. The vegetable kingdom feeds on the mineral kingdom directly.

That is why organic gardening and hydroponics don't clash. However, the distinction is that the soil is fed with dead plant and animal matter, not the plant, in organic gardening. Soil acts as a natural fertilizer factory that goes with its soil bacteria in league with weathering to operate on these organic substances. This breaks down these compounds into their inorganic components, so the plants can consume them.

To grow, a plant uses two simple processes. The first osmosis takes over the sources of water and minerals. The second, photosynthesis, converts water and minerals into plant tissue using light and atmosphere. To breathe, roots also need air, and that's one reason why hydroponics works so well. The loose, chunky growing medium of hydroponic growth, the aggregate as it is called, allows plenty of air to enter the roots. But to ensure proper aeration, natural soil also requires a lot of work and time.

There is no soil in hydroponics, and the plants are fed directly with the minerals provided by healthy organic soil. The plant does not know or care how man or nature made its mineral food. However, it is diligent that it is well fed, and nitrate is a nitrate, whether it comes from a solution of nutrients or a dead mouse.

Hydroponic gardening has four approaches:

1. Growing outdoors like farmers, but using a hydroponic system instead of soil

2. Indoor hydroponic development

3. A combination of these two, the garden

4. Throughout the year. Growing in a greenhouse hydroponically.

Many risk factors are minimized by monitoring the plant's climate. Plants cultivated in garden and fields are exposed to a variety of variables which affect their health and growth negatively. Soil mushrooms can transmit plant diseases. Fauna, such as rabbits, will loot your garden's mature vegetables. In the afternoon, plagues like sautéing will invade and kill them. The unpredictability of plants growing outside and on earth stopped with hydroponic systems. Seedlings can grow much faster without the mechanical resistance of the soil. Hydroponics is growing much more and healthier fruit and vegetables by removing pesticides. Plants can grow rapidly and quickly without obstacles.

Nutrients for The Plants

Nutrients are integral of your success because your plants need to be supplied with food continuously. You can mix your own nutrients in large or small amounts using the formulae shown herein. However, the novice should start with a commercially available, premixed nutrient at least until a hydroponic sensation has been established.

In soil farming, nature does a lot of work, although often not completely, otherwise, farmers would not have to use fertilizers. Nearly all soil has nutrients in it, but you take over from nature when you grow hydroponically, and often you can improve the quality of the nutrients supplied.

Nutrient Solution

Plants collect the nutrients they need to grow from the soil, and it may have been apparent to you already that in hydroponics, water supplies the nutrients. However, water alone doesn't have the 14 nutrients plants require, thus there is the need for nutrient solutions.

The first thing to know about nutrient solutions is that it comes in different ratios. Plants constantly change their requirements as they grow; thus, gardeners can't stick to a single solution throughout. Furthermore, different crops require different nutrient ratios. What will make a tomato crop bloom may not do the same for an orchid.

Nutrient solutions can be bought in hydroponics stores, and their ratios are clearly printed on the bottle's label - the three seemingly random numbers at the bottom (e.g. 2-1-6, 0-5-4, or 5-0-1). Each number stands for the three primary macronutrients, commonly known as NPK or nitrogen (N), phosphorus (P), and potassium (K). Although they are called 'ratios', these numbers are the percentages of each macronutrient against the entire bottle. Therefore, if the label says, 2-1-6, it means it contains 2% nitrogen, 1% phosphorus, and 6% potassium.

Homemade Nutrients

The most common homemade nutrient is made from salts extracted from fertilizer. Such salts are available in bulk from farm companies, suppliers of plant food, some nurseries, and gardening shops, and suppliers of chemicals. The only problem with this approach is that in twenty-five to fifty-pound bags, you generally have to buy some of these salts, and unless you grow in large hydroponic gardens, these amounts will make the whole thing very difficult and expensive.

Besides the three essential elements of nitrogen (N), phosphorus (P) and potassium (K) for all plant growth, your nutrient will contain at least ten trace elements. The following are sulfur, iron, manganese, zinc, copper, boron, magnesium, calcium, molybdenum, chlorine.

As fertilizer for the hydroponic culture, three different forms are used: nutrient salt, liquid fertilizer, or ion exchange fertilizer. Then it is subdivided according to the composition: nitrogen-stressed, phosphorous-retained, potassium-reinforced, etc., depending on the use of plants with special needs. The (normal) regulating fertilizer is slightly potassium-enriched and meets the needs of most ornamental and indoor plants. There are also fertilizers that contain only one nutrient or two or three nutrients. It is used when, for a short time or during a particularly needy growth phase (flowering), this single nutrient is needed to an increased extent.

The composition of a (normal) fertilizer is characterized by the three (or four) characters NPK. N is nitrogen (nitrogen), P is phosphorus, K is potassium. Often one finds on the label also the fourth sign mg, and it stands for magnesium. These characters are followed by numbers separated by a hyphen or colon. Example: NPKMG 123162 or 12: 3: 16: 2. It is the composition, in this case, a potassium-stressed fertilizer, which is mostly used for hydroponics. There are other compositions as well. Thus, in the hydroponic commercial horticulture in the first growth phase, a nitrogen-stressed fertilizer is often used in the bloom phase, a phosphorus-rich, and in the fruit phase a kaliumbetonter. Cacti usually need a specially made fertilizer, namely a more potassium-stressed (because of the strong water binding of the tissue). Another fertilizer contains little or no nitrogen. It is added to the nutrient solution only when the desired pH value has been determined. Namely, it can be influenced by selecting a particular nitrogen fertilizer type of ph. The addition of ammonium allows the lowering of the pH value, which, however, requires experience.

A disadvantage is the use of liquid hydroponic fertilizer and dissolved hydroponic fertilizer, as this shortened the cleaning interval of the vessels. Part of the fertilizer crystallizes out and settles in expanded clay. This should be rinsed with every renewal of the nutrient solution. Here's a word about so-called fertilizer. There is no artificial fertilizer! This is just the expression of people who lack understanding of manure and fertilizer. One should also speak better of mineral fertilizer.

The nutrient solution consists of water to which all nutrients necessary for plant growth are added. This sounds easier than it is. At this point, therefore, only the necessary is to be conveyed. Anyone who wants to know exactly can acquire all deepening knowledge under advanced hydroponics.

• Irrigation water

Proper fertilization depends on the particular water quality in each case. Depending on their location or origin, irrigation water may contain varying amounts of both beneficial and undesirable substances (ions). There is, therefore, no patent remedy for the fertilization of "hydroponics" incidentally, this also applies to all other culture processes, including those inorganic substrates. Simplified, the different waters can be divided into the following classes:

• Low salt with low conductivity and low hardness, including rainwater

• Medium salt content and medium hardness

- High salt content and high hardness

The water supply companies provide detailed information on tap water quality, either directly or via the internet. Beware of in-house water softening systems. These change the composition of the tap water considerably. Softened water is unsuitable as water for plants.

Chapter - 14
WHAT ARE THE BENEFITS OF HYDROPONICS?

Improved genetic health

Plants in a hydroponic system are not only provided with nutrition that has a near to perfect composition, but they're also safeguarded from many potential pests that they could otherwise meet when growing in soil. This allows the plants to reach a higher level of genetic health. As the saying goes, 'you are what you eat.'

High-scale production

Although hydroponics can be used to create your variety of plants at home, an often-surprising fact is that the hydroponic process is responsible for providing food to millions. The science has now been improved to a level at which more fruit, vegetables, and herbs can be produced at a higher quality than ever before! Yields from growing hydroponically are at least 20% greater than with growing with soil.

Affordable

Hydroponics will allow you to say goodbye to the often-costly ordeals of obtaining prepared soils and plant protection products. On top of this, most of the standard gardening tools (e.g. trowels, shovels, forks) are not needed.

Less-time, more produce

The process of planting becomes a breeze because you will no longer have to spend time preparing soil between planting. On top of this, your plants will be able to mature faster, generating you an abundance of beautiful produce.

Vegetables, fruits, and flowers grow healthier

With hydroponics, plants get the right kinds of nutrient in the right amounts at the right time, which means that they contain the correct nutrient values in the produce. Studies show that there is 50% more nutritive content in crops grown in hydroponic gardens in contrast to traditional ones.

Faster, better results are achieved

Since nutrients are introduced and adjusted in the water, the plants feed directly and do not expend much energy tracing and extracting needed supply of nutrients. They grow faster, bigger, and in superior quality. In this sterile, controlled environment, you will get double the yield from your crops.

Hydroponic gardens are easy to maintain

You can have a soil-less garden indoor or outdoor. You require less labor in the set-up and upkeep of a hydroponic garden. You don't need to test your soil or set up a plot. You can also use commercially available pH-balanced nutrient solutions.

You can grow and enjoy your crops

A lot of people worry about the chemical content in their food because of inorganic fertilizers, insecticides, and other plant sprays. Growing your vegetables and fruits at home can give you peace of mind that what you are eating is fresh and free from chemicals.

In a hydroponic garden, it is easy to harvest vegetables, fruits, and flowers. Moreover, you save more money.

You can grow plants anywhere

You only need a growing medium, water system, nutrient solution, and a light source, and you're good to go. Remember that plants will grow if their needs are met.

You save space

Unlike in soil gardens, you cannot have plants grow too close together or they will fight each other for nutrients. In a hydroponic garden, you can place plants with small roots together, and they will grow just as big and healthy as a traditional garden.

You help protect the environment

Traditional gardening leads to the degradation of soils as high amounts of potassium, phosphorus, and calcium are introduced to it through fertilizers. Hydroponics is a good way to reduce the amount of arable land.

Also, you need far less water for a hydroponic garden than you would in a soil-based one which contributes to conserving our Earth's water.

Hydroponic gardening is fun and relaxing

Hydroponic gardening is advantageous not only to commercial farmers but to home gardeners and those who are looking for hobbies, as well. Soil-less gardening is a fun, innovative, and great way to relax or spend time with your family. Additionally, there is much less physical labor involved in hydroponic gardening as compared to conventional gardening. It is a great stress reliever, as well. What can be more relaxing and rewarding than seeing the fruits of your labor literally, right in your own home?

There is little chance of environmental degradation

Fertilizers are not required in hydroponic farming. Additionally, you don't need to worry about changing seasons and weather conditions. Often, bad weather leads to the destruction of prized plants, flowers, and crops that you've worked so hard to cultivate, but with a hydroponic system you can avoid these natural disasters.

There is very little wastage of resources in hydroponic farming

Waste products are reduced because dirt and soil are not utilized. Water is easily disposed of in a clean and proper way. This reduces the possibility of over or under-watering. The supply of nutrient water is regulated; therefore, you will not have to double-check if the water is enough or not.

The money you invest in preparing a garden and maintaining it is returned through produce which you can eat or sell for profit.

Safer and less need for the use of pesticides and chemicals

With hydroponic gardening, you also eliminate the possibility of pest infestation, therefore also removing the use of pesticides. This leads to a much healthier garden and products.

Improved home environment

Hydroponic gardens are some of the most beautiful gardens to have in your home. You can drastically improve the look of your environment through hydroponic gardening. Just as the site of an aquarium in your house is breathtaking, so it is the site of plants in your home.

The relieved strain on your budget

Food is expensive, even more so are fresh fruits and vegetables. You can make a great cut in your household budget by simply utilizing your free space by having a hydroponic garden.

Enriched skills

A Hydroponic garden is not just a garden, but a botanical laboratory of its own kind. You get to learn a lot about plants – how to take care of them, their basic requirements and how to maximize yields. You also learn how to utilize your farming skills as you get exercise and learn how to create a scenic, green landscape around your compound.

When looking at the above advantages, you might be thinking, "Where's the catch?" There has to be a downside, here right. Otherwise, hydroponic growing would be more widespread and commonplace. Hydroponics can seem complicated at first, the thick veil of technical jargon scares many people away before they have the chance to discover just how simple it can be to start growing plants hydroponically.

Chapter - 15
WHAT ARE THE DRAWBACKS OF HYDROPONICS?

Requires Technical Knowledge and Experience

When running a hydroponics system, realize that you are running a system composed of many kinds of equipment, and this requires you to have specific expertise and knowledge of the devices you are to use, the plants you are to grow, and the mechanism of how these plants are to grow in the soilless environment. If you make mistakes in regard to setting up the systems or how you plan out your care of the crops, you may end up losing out on your investment.

There Are Risks Related to Electricity and Water

A hydroponics system primarily depends on water and electricity to operate. The combination of water and electricity, however, is a recipe for disaster, especially because they are used in such close proximity. Therefore, whenever you are working with electricity and the water systems equipment together, consider safety measures first.

The Initial Expenses Are Quite High

As you start out your hydroponics farm, you are sure to spend some considerable amount (the scale of your farming will also matter), to set up the space to be used for farming and to purchase the equipment needed. Whichever hydroponics system you take up, you will also need a pump, growing media, fertilizers, containers, lights, and seeds or seedlings.

Once your system is in place, you will only be paying for electricity, water, nutrients, and seedlings, as needed.

The Costs of Running Are Also Quite High

The control systems of the hydroponic garden, which would include the water purifiers, pumps, heaters, lights, and others, are electronically powered, and this costs money. In traditional farming, the water, the heat, and the light are naturally provided, and they are free, which makes them an added cost.

It Takes a While for You to Get a Return on Your Investment

Just recently, large scale hydroponic farms have been coming up, which shows that people now believe in the productivity of the soilless farms. That's a great development for agriculture and the development of hydroponics also. However, the issue is that the commercial growers setting up large-scale hydroponic farms will have to wait longer to receive a return on their investment.

The cost of setting up the large farms is particularly high, and the returns can be uncertain at times. As such, it would be difficult to come up with a profitable clear plan that would justify the investment while there are other attractive investment opportunities out there that would give a return on investment quicker, and more certainly than hydroponics farming.

Diseases and Pests Spread Quickly

Since you will be growing plants in a closed damp place, in the event that pests and infections come along, they can spread and escalate very fast among plants that are in the same nutrient reservoir.

In a small system, the pests or diseases would not cause so much havoc, which means that it is not quite a problem for beginners because you are advised to start small. For big farms, the issue could become problematic since the water is filtered and then recycled throughout the farm. Therefore, if a diseased plant is present in one portion of the farm, it will infect the remaining area and could kill the entire crop in hours. Many large-scale farmers have lost their entire crop this way, which has made disease-control one of the critical factors to look out for when investing in hydroponics. All farmers, particularly those operating on a large scale, ought to have a proper disease and pest management plan early enough.

One of the best preventative measures is to ensure cleanliness in the farm. For one, only use clean pathogen-free water and growing materials, clean and check the hydroponic systems periodically. In case the diseases occur, you need to sterilize the infected nutrients, water, and the entire hydroponic system.

The downside of this cleanliness and sterilization exercise is that the water might also contain good microorganisms, and unfortunately, when the water is sterilized, it is impossible to eliminate the harmful streaks of bacteria and fungi and leave out the good ones; they all go out in the same swipe. In addition, the sterility of the water and the entire farm at large is only as good as the sterilization method that the farmer uses; the water could retain some harmful microorganisms.

Threats of System Failure

Farmers use electricity to manage the entire system and should take precautionary measures to prepare for a possible power outage. This is because were there to be a power outage or electrical failure, the entire system would stop working immediately, and the plants would dry out quickly, and die in a matter of hours. Therefore, farmers ought to have ready plans to prepare for power-related issues by having a backup power source, particularly those operating under large-scale systems. Most farmers opt to have several long-standing back-up generators that can run for a long time in case of an electrical emergency.

The Organic Question

There have been debates on whether crops grown under hydroponic systems can be labeled as organic or not. Some people raised questions as to whether plants grown as hydroponics get microbiomes as those that are grown in the soil.

Whatever the case, the fact remains that people have grown hydroponic crops all over the world including tomatoes, lettuce, strawberries, and others, for many years, and distributing them to the Netherlands, the United States, Australia, Tokyo, and other regions. This product has fed millions of people, and it poses fewer risks in regard to pesticides, pests, and diseases, compared to soil-grown crops.

Some suggestions into how hydroponics growers can turn their agriculture into an organic venture have been laid out, and some farmers have taken up this idea. Some have gone ahead to introduce microbiomes to the soil in the form of organic growing media such as coco coir, then adding worm casting into it. Others introduce natural nutrients instead of fertilizer in the form of alfalfas, neems, cotton seeds, fishes, and bones.

As for the organic debate though, there is yet to be a consensus on what qualifies to be organic and what does not, and as research continues to be carried out, we can hope to have a conclusive answer in the near future.

Requires a Heavy Investment of Time and Commitment

Just like any other worthwhile thing in life that requires hard work and a positive attitude to obtain any success, hydroponics requires your utmost dedication to attain the success that you anticipated. Plants that are planted on soil do not demand as much attention and dedication and can be left alone for many days and weeks, and they will continue to grow. The soil, together with Mother Nature, balance out whatever needs balancing.

The case of hydroponics is different. If the plants do not receive all the care and attention they need, they begin to die out. The plants are purely dependent on the farmer for survival, which means that the farmer must be equipped with the proper knowledge and expertise to care for them. Initially, farmers are advised to care for the plants themselves, and they can automate at a later time, once the system is up and running.

Hydroponics Limit Agricultural Production

Although growing your crops all year round increases the yield significantly, the space available remains an impediment to the amount you could possibly produce. In addition, the fact that you can plant more crops in a single space does not mean that the crops can be overcrowded; the plant still needs some space to enable it spread out, which means that there is still a limited number of crops you can plant at a time.

The Entire Hydroponic System Is Quite Vulnerable

As mentioned earlier, it only takes a few hours without power and the plants begin to dry out and die. In a system where the plants are exposed, if the plants are left unwatered for some hours, the drying out will be especially quick.

In addition, it is more likely to have pH and nutrient imbalances when using a solution as their source in comparison to when you use soil. If these imbalances happen, an entire crop could be wiped out very fast, and so is the situation in case of water contamination by either microorganisms or disease.

Requires Some Knowledge and Expertise

A farmer who wishes to venture into hydroponic farming needs to understand the entire process and the techniques used, and this can be quite complicated to grasp.

As you have seen, hydroponics farming stands to give you a number of advantages but will still subject you to some disadvantages. If you still feel the need to press on and start your farm, go ahead and get started, there will always be a way around the challenges you face. Nothing should keep you from enjoying and selling to others the juicier, larger, tastier, and more nutritious foods you have been dying to try growing using the hydroponics method.

You also should ensure that you contact the local agricultural department to determine the requirements set for farm operations, as well as be informed of any existing risk of encountering fungi, bacteria, and other common diseases. Keep in mind that the most important lessons are learned by trial and error so that as you encounter challenges, you will keep learning and pushing yourself forward. In the end, your dream of successfully running a piece of this revolutionary method of agriculture will come to be.

Chapter - 16
CHOOSING THE RIGHT HYDROPONICS SYSTEM

Automation

There are lots of components that are used in the hydroponic system. These components include the pumps, lights, and some other essential components. These components are quite crucial in ensuring that the systems are highly automated. Automation is also an option for you to decide. Manual and automatic systems are both available, and it is your responsibility to choose.

Different recent researches have indicated that gardening failure that happens usually happens because of the reduced control of temperature and the levels of water. Hence getting a system that could be automated will do half of the work done. The decidedly more modern systems usually come with devices that can automatically check and regulate temperature, humidity, and water levels. Consequently, this takes half of the work from you.

Available Space

You also need to check the space that is available and how far you will be willing to create and install the hydroponic system. This is quite important because the available space will affect the quantity of buckets and pots that can possibly be installed in the hydroponic system. This then will affect the plants that will be grown on the site.

In several cases, small hydroponic systems will need a floor space of as much as 16 sq. ft. You will also need to have some more space that will be needed to place the water reservoir. There is also space needed for the lighting, coolers, and pump. Hence before you begin, you should be able to analyze the space you can get for the system.

Energy efficiency

Each of the hydroponic system that you may choose uses electricity, and this supports the pumping, lighting, and the air. The cost of electricity can be a high burden, especially when the materials that are used are not energy friendly. Using energy-saving LED bulbs can be better. A better spectrum of light is what is required so that the system can come out in the best condition for the plant.

Hence when you purchase your hydroponic system, you should make sure to utilize the energy-saving LED bulbs as this will last you a long time and reduce the expenses that come with operating the system.

Expandability

As a person who wants to begin hydroponics, you may want to start with a smaller kit, and then if it becomes favorable, you will want to expand your gardening much later. As soon as you convince yourself of the merits of having a hydroponic farm, then you will want to increase the scope of the system so that you can benefit more.

In cases where you want to expand, then you will need to have functional space so you can hold more buckets or pots as these can help you effectively hold other plants. This factor determines the output, and it is a very important consideration that can help you make an outstanding choice for the system.

Crops

The crops you are going to be planting should also be factored in, as this can affect the system you are going to use. What is the optimum temperature of the crops you want to grow, and, you have to consider if the crops are small or large stature? A crop that is quite large when it is matured will need to be grown on a hydroponic that can hold it firmly. It, therefore, means that aeroponics is not the best option for this kind of crop since it doesn't have a firm media for it.

Facility

You should consider the layout, utilities, and all the environmental factors. You will have to check if you will need to work with pillars, small rooms; also, you will need to be in a facility that can deal with fluctuation in temperature.

Also, you can check the labor and how efficient you want your labor to be. Consider how many persons you want to be in the facility.

Costs of setting up the system

There are different costs to set up the different types of hydroponic systems, and this can be another factor that can affect your choice. They can be purchased as ready-made, and you can also construct one yourself. Constructing yourself will make you need a professional, and this can affect your cost because if you do not have any idea how to make it, then you will hire a professional to help you construct.

This can be quite expensive for those beginning, and it will need proper monitoring, especially during installation.

You could also get an already made from the market as the market is filled with lots of already built system, and then any of these already built system could be customized to meet your needs. With these systems, you can begin your gardening just right away.

And then with just your budget determining it, you can decide to build your hydroponics, or you get an already made system from the market.

Chapter - 17
MAINTENANCE OF YOUR HYDROPONIC GARDEN

These are tips and tricks from experienced growers who have experimented a lot over the years and want you to be as successful as they are.

1. If you are looking to build your hydroponics system from recycled material, do not forget to check out Craigslist. So many people do their best to give away the things they do not need, and you may even find an entire hydroponics system for free or for a very low price. You should also check out the local yard sale sites and you will want to check out local yard sales. Hydroponics systems can be made out of anything that you find around your house or at local sales; all you have to do is be a bit creative and look for the system that works for you.

2. If you do not want to keep your hydroponics system in the house and you do not want to worry about your plants getting enough light, you can set up your hydroponics system in a greenhouse. Greenhouses are very easy to put together and you can purchase small ones for quite cheap if you do not have a lot of space. Having a greenhouse is going to take the hydroponics system out of your house, ensure that your plants are getting the right amount of

light, and reduce your issues with humidity. If you do want to use a greenhouse, you need to consider how you will get electricity to your system. You need to think about this in advance so that you do not get your entire system set up in your greenhouse and then realize that you do not have any way to get electricity to your system.

3. Make sure that you know the equipment you will need for your system and why you will need it. I hope I have done a good job at explaining what you will need for your system and why you will need it, but you need to know this because not knowing your system is one of the reasons many people fail at hydroponics. Many people think that they can take shortcuts with their system, cutting out vital equipment that the system needs, and soon they find out that the system will not work the way they thought it would. This often leads to discouragement and the person will give up on hydroponics, blaming the system for the issues and not realizing that they did not follow the directions. Make sure you follow the directions when it comes to your system and the equipment you will need.

4. Use a three-part hydroponics nutrient solution. The three-part nutrient solution is going to be the best for your plants, providing the right nutrients in the correct proportions. Your nutrient solution is very important when it comes to the growth and health of your plants. If you do not provide your plants with the best nutrient solution possible, you are going to find that your plants do not do well, and your yields are going to be very low.

5. You should not keep your hydroponics garden outside unless the temperature is above 55° F. The great thing about a hydroponics system is that it can be moved outdoors in the summer months and indoors during the winter months. This means that you are going to be able to have healthy, fresh fruits and vegetables all year round. It is also a great idea to grow the summer foods during the summer months, when the growing season is ending, clean

your system, move it into the house and plant the fall foods. This will not only give you a variety of foods, but it will mean that you have less to worry about when it comes to maintaining specific temperatures for your system.

6. Check your nutrient reservoir every day. If you have a pump in your system, you need to check the pump on a regular basis because if your pump stops working, your entire system can collapse within a few hours, but you also need to check the levels of your nutrient solution. If you do find that the levels are low, simply add some extra water to the reservoir. You do not want to add extra nutrient solution because the nutrients can build up on the roots of the plants and cause a toxic environment. Also, if you are continually adding nutrient solutions to your reservoir, the nutrients will never deplete, and you will never have a good time to clean your system.

7. When you are cleaning your system, you need to move quickly. It is important to clean the inside of the reservoir to ensure that algae do not grow in it and deplete your nutrient solution, but you do not want to allow your plants to dry you either. Cleaning the system needs to be done at least once every 10 days and it can be something that can cause a bit of dread because of the amount of speed that is needed to clean it but once you get into a routine, it will get much easier. I would advise that before you start, you get all of your supplies together, that way you do not have to run around gathering your supplies while your plants have no nutrient-rich solution available to them.

8. Minimize the amount of light that reaches your nutrient-rich solution. The light is what will allow the algae to grow. If a lot of light is reaching your solution, you will have many problems with algae, you will have to clean your reservoir more and you will be wasting a ton of your nutrients and doing nothing more than feeding algae.

9. Stay out of your garden after you have been in another garden or if you have been outside. This is especially true if you have your garden indoors. I stated earlier that you will not have to worry about bugs because there is no soil, but if you are in another garden that does have bugs, they can hang on to your clothes and make their way to your garden, completely destroying your plants in no time. Instead, shower and change your clothes before visiting your garden, just to make sure that you do not bring any little hitchhikers' home with you to your healthy garden.

Most Common Problems and Mistakes and How to Avoid Them

If you are simply beginning with your hydroponic nursery, you need to take things moderate and simple. One misstep can crush all the advancements you have made on your development. Rather, set aside the effort to comprehend what your plants anticipate from you and the conditions they need.

Numerous issues can emerge in a hydroponic nursery, however, here are the 5 most-normal missteps a hydro cultivator can make:

The pH is the most important estimation for hydroponic nurseries

Error 1 – IGNORING PH LEVELS

The most important estimation for your hydroponic framework is its pH level. Generally, your plants exist as a rule because of a supplement arrangement. If that arrangement is excessively antacid or excessively acidic, your plants will encounter supplement inadequacies or just kick the bucket.

Get yourself a choice pH meter and screen the levels at any rate once per day. If it slides toward some path, find a way to bring it again into the equalization your plants need.

A helter-skelter pH level is one of the most well-known explanations behind plant bite the dust offs in a hydroponic framework. It is unimaginably critical to screen pH levels because every one of your plants lives in a similar supplement arrangement – if your pH is terrible for one plant, every one of your plants could endure!

Without the correct lighting, hydroponic plants will not endure

Error 2 – BUYING CHEAP, INCORRECT OR NOT ENOUGH LIGHTING

Putting resources into the correct lighting can represent the deciding moment of your hydroponic nursery! If you purchase pretty much nothing, your plants will endure. If you purchase an inappropriate sort of bulb for your plants, they will not develop. If you pick to purchase the least expensive bulbs, they may not perform.

Lighting is one of the most significant speculations you will make as a hydroponic cultivator, so search out the best for your harvest! This implies you should inquire about the sort of light your plants will require because different bulbs put out different vitality types.

Additionally, do not anticipate that your plants should flourish if they are set beside a window. That light is often not sufficiently able to fuel the incredible development you anticipate from a hydroponic plant.

Hydroponic Gardens require certain plant nourishment

Slip-up 3 – USING THE WRONG PLANT FOOD

It very well may be enticing to purchase a sack of manure from your neighborhood garden community for use in your hydroponic framework. Overall, it is tied in with conveying supplements, isn't that so?

Not really! Customary manure may not weaken totally through your framework. Similarly, it can obstruct depletes and tubes. Rather, put resources into manure intended for hydroponic frameworks. Hydroponic compost, which is accessible as fluids or granules, meets the developing prerequisites you need in a soil-less or soil-light nursery by giving extra supplements your plants may somehow or another miss.

Poor sanitation can prompt develop room vermin and plant maladies

Mix-up 4 – NOT FOCUSING ON SANITATION

Try not to let your hydroponic nursery region become a trash canister. Your sanitation propensities can majorly affect the soundness of your plants and your whole hydroponic framework.

Some essential cleaning needs that you should address:

Keeping floors spotless and dry

- Disinfecting and cleaning framework hardware
- Disinfecting and cleaning devices
- Disinfecting and cleaning holders
- Discarding plant squander

Without appropriate sanitation, you can spread plant infection or furnish bothers with concealing spots and sustenance.

New data on Hydroponic Gardening is accessible constantly

Error 5 – OPTING NOT TO LEARN

Current hydroponic frameworks have been around since the mid-twentieth century, and in that time, a great deal of data and direction has been made accessible. School courses are educated on it. Many books are accessible.

To put it plainly, don't go only it! Peruse up and arrange your hydroponic nursery. Converse with other hydroponic cultivators and offer thoughts. The more you know before setting up your nursery, the happier you will be when you are prepared to reap.

Chapter – 18
MANAGING PESTS AND PLANT DISEASES

Insect pests and plant diseases are part of the challenges every gardener dread to face in their garden, but more often than not, they attack and damage the plants in the garden. The activities of these pests and diseases vary from garden to garden. For example, they tend to strike a traditional garden more than they do in containers. But keep in mind that planting in container does not completely eliminate the presence of pests and diseases; it only limits their attack. This means that there is still a tendency, no matter how little, that your plants will get attacked by pests and diseases. It is, therefore, necessary to be equipped with the knowledge of how to fight these menaces in case your plants get infected. If you are not growing plants from the seed level, it is essential to ensure that the young plants you purchase are free of pests before planting them in your garden. Because that is one of the easiest ways to spread infection in a container garden, especially when you grow plants vertically. Managing pests and plant diseases in your garden begins from you learning to monitor your garden. You can only fight what you know to exist. Knowing signs of pests and disease infections early in your plants is the key to having a successful container garden. Identifying the common pests that attack plants and how they operate will help in fighting against them and maintaining a healthy garden.

Pests

1. Aphids

Aphids are soft-bodied insects that feed on tender growing tips and underside of leaves. Although they are small, they are capable of causing stunted and distorted growth in plants. Examples of plants that get affected easily include hibiscus, ivy, dahlia, chrysanthemum, etc.

2. Caterpillars and Snails

Infestation from caterpillars can damage a plant if not identified early. Caterpillars can simply be picked off the plants' surface. Snails can also be very troublesome as they can cause severe damage to the garden. They are known to feast on plants at night while they hide behind containers during the day. Snails and caterpillars avoid sunlight and dry weather, and as a result, they almost go unnoticed until the damage they have done becomes very glaring. Caterpillars often eat leaves from the edges while snails cut holes in the middles of the leaves. Hanging baskets are usually free of snails.

3. Mealybugs

Mealybugs look like spots of cottony white mold. They can be found on the roots, stems, and leaves of plants. If not detected early enough, they are capable of causing damages such as stunted growth and early leaf drop in plants. Commonly affected plants include; coleus, African violets, gardenia, cacti, succulents, etc.

4. Whiteflies

Whiteflies are tiny gnat-like insects that are small and white in color. They flutter and swarm in clouds when disturbed. Signs of affected plants include leaf drop, yellowing, etc. They often feast on plants such as; eggplant, okra, sweet potatoes, peppers, etc.

5. Soft scales

These pests attach themselves to the leaves, twigs, trunks, foliage, and stems of plants. They usually secrete a waxy coating on the plant' leaves, which are not removable. They affect mostly ornamental plants.

6. Thrips

These insects are tiny; they affect plants by causing streaking and distortion of flowers and foliage. Thrips usually feed on flowers and the undersurface of leaf tissue. The buds of affected plants often fail to open. Examples of plants they feed on include; vegetables, grapes, strawberries, peaches, pomegranate, etc.

7. Vine weevils

These pests eat the roots of plants. A plant attacked by vine weevils is usually wholly damaged, and it is vital that the soil is discarded and never reused. Plants mostly affected by vine weevil include; Bergenia, cyclamen, sedum, phlox, heuchera, aster, azalea, etc.

8. Red spider mites

These tiny arachnids thrive in hot and dry conditions. They feast on the underside of leaves and commonly affect plants like; ivy, Schefflera, figs, hibiscus, camellias, azaleas, etc. Signs to looks out for include mottling of leaves, fine webs at the underside or on plant's branches, discoloration, dusty appearance to the bottom of the plant's leaves, and early leaf drop.

While many of these pests may not be easily spotted on the plants, pests such as aphids, mealybugs, soft scales, and whiteflies all give sticky body waste of honeydew when they feed. A sign of honeydew on your plant can be a sign that your plant is under pest attack. After getting familiar with the common pests that affect garden plants, it is now essential to learn how to fight them and maintain a healthy garden as much as possible.

Controlling Pests

The methods used in controlling pests and diseases in container plants include;

- Handpicking: large pests like caterpillars, snails, etc. can easily be handpicked when spotted on the plants.

- Rinsing: you can manage pests by rinsing the leaf of affected plants with warm water.

- Contact insecticides: apply contact insecticide to the infected part(s) of the plants.

- Pruning: you can also simply trim off the part of the plant that is infected

- If the infected part of the plant is an area that cannot be easily reached, use cotton swabs dipped in alcohol to reach the affected spot.

- Horticultural oil can also be used to fight pest attack

- Isolate the affected plant(s) to avoid spread among other plants

- Disinfect the pruners you use with isopropyl alcohol or a bleach solution (9 part of water, 1 part of bleach)

Diseases

Pest attacks are somewhat easier to manage than disease attacks in gardens, but disease attacks don't happen as often as pest attacks do. Common diseases that affect plants include;

1. Powdery mildew

This disease forms a white powdery coating tinged with grey on the leaves and stems of the plants. Signs of powdery mildew include distortion in plants' growth.

2. Gray mold

This disease usually affects flowers and foliage. Signs of this disease include dusty gray spores on leaf tissue, brown and wet spots on flowers.

3. Root rot

This disease is often the result of excess water in the root system of plants or damaged roots. It causes the roots of plants to wilt. It can be identified by the presence of brown roots, which is contrary to the firm and white root expected of every healthy plant. If root rot is left untreated, it is capable of killing the affected plant completely. The affected plant can only be saved if some parts of the root system are still white and firm. Commonly affected plants are succulents, cyclamen, and orchids.

4. Leaf spot fungus

This is a disease that affects the leaves of plants like palms and orchids. An oval brown spot with a yellow halo is often seen as a sign, and it can quickly spread to other healthy leaves through airborne spores. Creating good air circulation for the affected plant is one of the ways to restore the affected plant.

Managing Plant Diseases

When it comes to pests and diseases in gardening, prevention is always better than managing, but just like sicknesses in humans, we can do everything right and still fall sick. Keeping proper hygiene in your garden is an excellent preventive measure against plant diseases, but once in a while, the plants might get infected. The control measures to effectively manage plants' diseases in your garden include;

- Creating sufficient air circulation for the plants in your garden. Ensure that you avoid congestion as much as possible and ensure proper aeration in your growing medium as well.

- Maintaining a clean and healthy environment. This also helps to keep diseases far away from your plants. Ensure that your garden tools and containers are well sanitized and rid of any possible infection so that they do not become mediums through which infection is communicated to your plants.

- Watering your plants is excellent but doing it a little too much can be a problem. Water your plants according to the need and requirement of your plants. If you are using an automated watering system, ensure your containers have good drainage as well to avoid excess water accumulating in your soil. A damp soil with poor drainage is the beginning of trouble.

- Avoid growing too many plants together in a single container. Companion planting is great, but overcrowding is not healthy for your garden. Be sure to be moderate when practicing mixed farming.

- There are some diseases that once they affect your plant, they can rarely be treated. Isolate such a plant immediately rather than treat the plant in your garden to prevent further spread of the disease.

Ultimately, managing pests and diseases in your garden begin with you being sensitive and on the lookout for signs so that you can take the necessary action to fight the pests and diseases once you have identified them. Monitoring your garden as frequently as possible will enable you to be sensitive to the changes that happen on your farm. As a result, pests and diseases cannot thrive in your garden before you discover them.

Conclusions

Container gardening is really a lot like traditional gardening, but your plant is portable. If the pots are small enough and light enough, you can even avoid early season hail and other major storm complications that would otherwise ruin plants. Just bring them indoors on off days and set them back out when the weather is nice. You'll get some amazing fruit that way!

In addition to being more versatile, container gardening also requires a lot less soil than the traditional style of in-ground gardening. To utilize your containers as much as possible, try to follow the square foot gardening method. You can plant nine bean plants in one square foot, so you should be able to plant nine in a large pot!

Growing our own food is unquestionably among the most helpful pastimes in our own lives. We develop food in our garden, crop it and consume it minutes after. Raised together with our own hands, cooked and prepared thickly -- what more can we wish for? Most of us are aware of the health benefits of vegetables. You could even clap your shoulders in cutting air miles. There's surely no petroleum wasted in importing vegetables which come from throughout the world.

When we develop our own food, we understand exactly what's gone into developing it. Lots of men and women worry about pesticide residues in food. Even if science demonstrates these pesticide residues from foods are totally harmless since they're under a threshold, a lot of individuals simply prefer to consume food which has raised naturally with no artificial inputs and hopefully raised by themselves. Personally, I'm a dedicated organic gardener and I never utilized synthetic fertilizers or synthetic pesticides and that I believe there's not any demand for this. Nature itself takes care of this. As an older gardening buddy said: 'Plants only need to grow'.

From the backyard to the table, organic vegetable gardening from your home is one of the most satisfying and enduring efforts you can undertake. Planning a garden, preparing the soil, nurturing plants, outsmarting pests, harvesting, preserving, and preparing meals are many of the numerous benefits to both body and soul that come out of such an endeavor. Not only are you contributing to the health and well-being of yourself, your friends, and your family, but you are also actively participating in creating a healthier environment and a better world.

I hope you have appreciated this journey through the seasons and now have the confidence and knowledge to begin your own backyard garden. Advice on how to set up a garden; how to prepare the soil; how—and when and what—to plant; how to combat pests and diseases; how to harvest and preserve; how to succession plant to ensure continuous garden growth: these tips, techniques, recipes, and more are all here. In addition, the many positive reasons— from avoiding petrochemicals and their detrimental effects to the fostering of tastier and more nutritious food—for undertaking an organic garden are outlined throughout.

Take pleasure in growing your own plant, vegetable or flower for whatever purpose you have in mind. The benefits are numerous, and the downsides are so few. It is truly worth the effort. You may be asking why should you have a container gardening? Find out today!

Printed by Amazon Italia Logistica S.r.l.
Torrazza Piemonte (TO), Italy